Once every week, over NBC's national TV and radio network, some twenty million men, women and children become the audience for a show called "People Are Funny." Five times every week, over the CBS TV and radio network, another audience, estimated at six million people daily, enjoys a show entitled "House Party."

This has been going on for years and these two amazingly popular and long-lived shows have one thing in common—

ART LINKLETTER!

This amazing master of ceremonies, one of the most popular of all TV and radio personalities, is also a best-selling author.

His new hit is *The Secret World of Kids*. The one before that was called *Kids Say the Darndest Things!* And once upon a time he wrote another—this one.

PEOPLE ARE FUNNY was originally published by Doubleday & Company, Inc., at $2.50.

PEOPLE
ARE
FUNNY

BY ART LINKLETTER

INTRODUCTION BY BING CROSBY
ILLUSTRATED BY REISIE LONETTE

CARDINAL EDITION

POCKET BOOKS, INC. • NEW YORK

This CARDINAL edition has been revised from the original hard-bound edition and a new final chapter has been written by the author especially for Pocket Books, Inc. It is printed from brand-new plates made from completely reset, clear, easy-to-read type.

PEOPLE ARE FUNNY

Doubleday edition published September, 1947

CARDINAL edition published August, 1960
1st printing.....................June, 1960

L

CARDINAL editions are distributed in the U.S. by Affiliated
Publishers, Inc., 630 Fifth Avenue, New York 20, N.Y.

Dedication

To all of the good sports who have let me pry into their private lives, hit them with pies, kid their mothers-in-law, third-degree them, douse them in tanks, tease them with prizes, chase them with alligators, auction off their clothes, fool them with gags, and send them on wild-goose chases . . .

My thanks for helping me prove that in a world steeped in bitterness and suspicion . . . Americans retain that most precious of all qualities: the ability to have a good laugh at themselves!

Contents

INTRODUCTION BY BING CROSBY ix

"PEOPLE ARE FUNNY" 1

WEATHER REPORT: "BRAINSTORMS IN THE WEST" 20

FUN IN BEDLAM 43

HEIGH-HO! COME TO THE FAIRS! 65

ONE FOOT IN HEAVEN 88

STARS DON'T ALWAYS TWINKLE 105

MAKING LOVE TO FOUR HUNDRED PEOPLE 122

PEOPLE ARE STILL FUNNY 132

THE "HOUSE PARTY": THE KIDS 166

THE "HOUSE PARTY": THE GROWN-UP KIDS 179

MY SLIPS WERE SHOWING 194

THE POSTMAN RINGS MORE THAN TWICE 208

"THROUGH THE LOOKING GLASS" 224

Introduction

THE FACT THAT A BACKWARD FELLOW LIKE MYSELF IS writing a foreword for a book is proof that Art Linkletter can get people to do anything. Further, with the exception of Art, Bob Hope is the only other book writer I know. (My bookmaker friends, however, are legion.)

The success of the "People Are Funny" program seems to be "everybody wants to get into the act," and Art lets them in—with a vengeance.

Yes, we all like to let our hair down, and as Lady Godiva once proved, it is sometimes necessary. We are all inclined to show off. There was the time that my four sprouts amassed enough cabbage to buy themselves bicycles. Said money was earned by selling newspapers. (Every morning they'd fly from the hay, dash to the front porch, snatch the morning paper, and hold it for ransom.)

Anyhow, the little burglars wheeled their bikes up front of the shack for a demonstration. The first time around the house they yelled: "Look, Dad, no hands!" On the second trip around their cry was: "Look, Dad, no teeth!" My alarm was brief, for I realized that in the not-far-distant past I had done the same thing myself—and, as I recall, I threw in a busted collarbone for good measure.

People Are Funny—innately, consciously, and sometimes even unconsciously.

As for Linkletter himself, the lad who dreams up many of

the mad antics and lethal pranks for we the funny people to perform on his show, it must be said in all fairness that he suffers from astigmatism of the skull. This malicious malady distorts his brain, twists his reflexes, and gives him more notions than a five-and-ten-cent store.

A chemical analysis of Link would no doubt disclose that he has the imagination of Paul Bunyan, the determination of a salmon heading upstream to spawn, the intestinal fortitude of a stage mother, the diplomacy of Disraeli, and the viewpoint of the Divvil Himself.

So now, read on how Art and people cavort and carry on for laughs. It will prove that People Are Funny—but one thing still puzzles me: Is Linkletter a people?

—BING CROSBY

People
Are Funny

"People Are Funny"

It is 7:30 P.M. in the Art Linkletter theater on Vine Street in the heart of Hollywood.

The red light flashes on. The NBC producer hurls an excited cue. I shout into the microphone, *"Peepull Are Funny!"* A bald, bespectacled, middle-aged man on stage raises his arms to signal the opening applause . . .

His pants fall off. And, as the crowd roars, another half hour of premeditated madness takes the air.

Is there anyone in the audience who will kiss a live pig on the nose for fifty dollars? It seems that a hundred and fifty wildly waving men and women are not only willing but dying to do it. I pick the first man. He'll kiss a pig for fifty. He'll kiss a pig for forty. He'll kiss a pig for thirty. But he won't kiss a pig for twenty-five. He's wise to me.

Is there anyone in the audience who will kiss a pig for twenty-five dollars? Sixty hands still wave frantically. I select a woman. She'll kiss a pig for twenty-five. She'll kiss it for twenty. She'll do it for seventeen. But she won't do it for fifteen.

I switch again to a man. Down goes the price . . . ten, nine, eight, seven. He knows I've got him where I want him and he gets stubborn. Seven is his limit.

By this time the audience is shouting advice. "Don't let Linkletter trap you." "Don't go any cheaper." "Don't be a chump." "You'll be sorry!" An ex-marine will do it for five, four, three, two, a dollar. He'll do it for fifty cents, forty, thirty. The crowd is yelling like demons. The honor of the average man is at stake.

He kissed the pig for five cents! People Are Funny!

Twenty million people throughout the United States and Canada enjoy such zany stunts every week; screwball experiments built on the theory that people are more fun than anybody.

It's sort of frightening: The thought of twenty million people waiting each week to see what you'll do, what you'll say, and how you'll extricate yourself from an obviously bad jam. That's enough people to swing a presidential election, more people than attend football games played by every college in the country during an entire season, even more people than are on the government pay roll!

I paused to think about those twenty million fans one day. There they sit every Friday night, complacently enjoying the misfortunes of our contestants in the comparative safety of their own homes. They know they aren't going to receive a pie in the face or a quart of seltzer water on their heads. Smug, that's what they are! So I called a meeting of the clan. Our objective was to devise a joke we could play on twenty million people!

A few weeks later we signed off our show with this announcement: "Be sure to tune in next week, folks, when we'll have a sensational program. Our special guests will be Joan Crawford, Jimmy Stewart, Ann Sheridan, Robert Taylor, and Charles Boyer."

All over the country people canceled dinner dates, visits to relatives, trips to the movies. They stayed home to hear their favorites. Well, the following week we had Joan Crawford, Jimmy Stewart, Ann Sheridan, Robert Taylor, and Charles Boyer on the show, all right. Jimmy was sixty-four years old and worked in the maintenance department of a Hollywood hospital. Ann owned and operated a beauty shop. Bob Taylor and Chuck Boyer both worked at Lockheed Aircraft. Joan was a housewife. We'd found all of them in the Los Angeles telephone directory and there they were . . . as advertised!

When the trick was first exposed, a groan echoed from Maine to California. But it was followed by a coast-to-coast laugh as the audience realized what we had done to them. Today even the folks in Sauk Center twitch nervously when "People Are Funny" is on the air; *no one* is safe!

Is there some secret recipe for concocting an "idea" show which year after year lures millions of fans? Not at all. We're simply giving the average man a chance to see himself as others see him. That's a formula that can't lose.

"People Are Funny" is not the usual pretentious band wagon loaded with stars that you might expect to hear from Hollywood. There are no actors, no musicians, very few guest stars, and no written gags. In fact, the whole charm of the fun lies in the extreme poverty of trappings and the emphasis on plain everyday people. What they do and what they say when they're put on the spot provides more original humor and entertainment than the combined works of Oscar Wilde, Irvin S. Cobb, and Mark Twain. The contestant is "you" and "me" in our off-guard moments, and, as such, he is the most laughable, lovable guy in the world. He's Joe Shirtsleeve, the star of the show!

According to psychologists, in each of us there is hidden a secret ambition to say or do crazy things. Like walking into a china store and sweeping an armful of cups and saucers to the floor, or smashing a pie in a stranger's face, or walking into a big bar without a dime and yelling, "The drinks are on me, pardners!"

We've sent contestants out to do every one of those zany jobs. And even if you wrinkle your nose at some of the wilder stunts, you'll have to admit deep down that at least once in every show we score a bull's-eye on one of your own suppressed desires.

I've often thought of my psychology professor at college, Harry W. Steinmetz. If he could spend a few weeks with me and observe the causes and effects around one of our broadcasts, he'd give his books and his theories and his research material to the scrap-paper people and take up some reasonable profession, like tree surgery.

When people are confronted by a TV camera or microphone, they just don't react according to the books. There's a strangely fatalistic air about them when they parade up to do their stuff; a half-scared, half-wild look in their eyes. A psychiatrist might diagnose it as some kind of self-hypnotism.

But I do know that in nineteen years I've never had a refusal or even a tiny balk from any of my contestants. I've asked them to commit everything from a public strip tease to grand larceny and not one soul has turned me down. It scares me. The only answer I can find is that there is a streak of the extrovert in all of us that suddenly, without warning, pops up when we least expect it.

I'm always amused at volunteers during the period before the broadcast when I make my selections. I'll ask for contestants, and out of a studio audience of four hundred people at least half will shoot their hands skyward and wave frantically, hands that belong to people who ordinarily would shy modestly away from wearing a bathing suit in their own back yards. Yet those same people will break their necks to get on a stage and be dunked in a horse trough for the entertainment of countless strangers. It happens every week. (I'm glad it does!)

And the hand that waves most frantically when I ask for volunteers naturally attracts my attention and chances are I'll call on its owner. The expression on the face of the hand-waver, during the period of hand-waving, is an eager, excited, pleading one. But when I suddenly point to that hand-waver and say: "Okay, we'll take you," the look on his face changes as if he's just been hit by a bean ball. Dazedly he'll point to himself and murmur, "Me?"

Then he files out of his row of seats and nervously and

self-consciously comes to the stage. I know from experience exactly what's passing through his mind.

"What on earth should I do with my hands?" They've suddenly become as big as casseroles. A woman will invariably fondle a purse or pick a handkerchief to shreds; a man usually sticks them in his pockets and gets them out of the way as soon as possible.

"What sort of expression should I wear?" The customary one is a semi-sickly smile as the volunteer screws up his determination to be a good sport and go through with what he's started if it kills him.

"Are my stockings twisted?" Naturally the ladies are concerned about their appearance on stage. Small matter to them if they're face to face with disaster; they want to look their best before the other women in the audience. Men seldom bother to straighten a tie or smooth a wrinkled coat; they're too busy being brave. But women can always be counted upon, the second they reach the stage, to straighten a girdle, adjust a hat, or pat a wave into place.

"Should I show 'em I'm a comedian?" It occurs to everyone unaccustomed to public performances to feel that the audience expects him to show remarkable talents. Fortunately it is only a fleeting thought and the ordinary contestant quickly decides to be himself.

"Migawd! What am I *doing* up here?" They've just spent a lifetime crossing the stage and are now standing in front of the cameras, confronted by the sudden horrid thought that there can be no turning back. It is the last thought they have that they can call their own. From then on, I take over. They're given so much to do there's no time left to worry about the future.

Here is a classic example of how far people will go once they have volunteered to leave the safety of their seats in the crowd.

This elaborate gag was built around the famous wild-animal trainer Clyde Beatty, his huge iron cage, and three of his nastiest, snarlingest, hungriest lions.

A portable cage, fifteen feet high, thirty feet long, and twenty feet across, had been erected behind the backdrop on our NBC stage. The lions entered and departed from the cage through a small trap door at one end. From there they went up a ramp and into a special wagon. During the time I selected volunteers the main curtain was drawn and the studio audience had no idea of the menagerie concealed behind it. I held my breath in fear that the occasional snarls to my rear would tip off what was coming, but the audience never dreamed that those coughing rumbles from backstage belonged to three nervous lions.

We kept our secret well. My victim was a young in-

surance salesman. Optimistic, bright, cheerful—he never had a chance.

I asked him about his hobbies and what he did with his spare time. Then I asked him if he'd developed any new interests lately. He admitted he hadn't. That was the answer I was waiting for.

"Everyone should develop new interests," I enthused. "It keeps you alive and happy. No one should ever allow himself to stagnate . . . learn something new with each passing hour!" My contestant nodded in hearty agreement. And with that nod the curtains parted, revealing the big, empty, iron-barred enclosure.

"Does this equipment suggest anything to you?" I wanted to know.

"No," gulped the salesman nervously. "It sure doesn't!"

"It doesn't?" I echoed his words in mock amazement. "That's strange. It did to *us*. Yes sir! It just filled me with dandy new ideas for hobbies!" I paused to let the significance of those words take hold; then: "But don't worry. We have the finest man in the business to teach you all about this new hobby: Clyde Beatty, the noted lion and tiger trainer!"

With this introduction, Mr. Beatty appeared, bowed with a flourish, and stepped into the cage.

"In just a moment," I continued, "the great cats will be let into the cage and Mr. Beatty will demonstrate how much fun it is to train wild animals." I handed our contestant a pad and pencil. "You take notes as Mr. Beatty explains what he's doing, so that you'll know what it's all about when you get *your* chance."

"Yes . . . but—"

"Don't you worry, sir," I rushed on. "No harm can come to you, because we're going to give you the same whip, chair, and gun filled with blanks that Mr. Beatty is using. Then you just follow the notes you're about to take down, and there'll be nothing to it. Is it a deal?"

There was a terrified edge to his voice. "Well, Mr. Link-letter, I don't want to be a bum sport, but gosh—"

"Tell you what"—I was suddenly "inspired"—"will you do it if I first get a woman volunteer right out of the studio audience to do it *before* you do? How's that for a sporting proposition?"

It was a straw and he grabbed it fast. "Okay, but she's got to be in there when the lions are there too!"

"Of course. We wouldn't trick you like *that!*" And we wouldn't either, not like *that!*

Sitting in the audience, and ready to volunteer for the job, was *Mrs.* Clyde Beatty, a beautiful, young, blond animal trainer who had no more fear of walking into a cage full of lions than her famous husband. She was sitting in a pre-arranged seat, waiting to raise her hand when I called for volunteers among the women.

The lions were brought into the cage. The whip cracked and popped. Beatty talked into a microphone suspended from the top of the cage, explaining each movement to our perspiring volunteer and to the listening audience. He did it expertly, rapidly, and the lesson in lion taming was over in two minutes.

Stepping out of the cage, Beatty handed his whip, chair, and gun to the insurance salesman. He smiled encouragingly as he added: "All right, you're all set to go!"

"Wait a minute!" yelled the contestant. "What about the lady first?"

"Oh yes! We did promise you that, didn't we?" I recalled quickly. Then, turning to the studio audience, I confidently asked: "Is there a lady in the audience who will go into the cage with the lions for a dollar?" I waited for Mrs. Beatty's hand to go up.

Then came the bombshell. Hands went up all over the place!

There were wrinkled old hands from ladies in lavender and lace, pink young hands from bobby-soxers; fat hands, thin hands, long hands, short hands. They all waved frantically . . . women dying to say "hello" on a coast-to-coast show and willing to walk into a cage of snarling lions as the price for the privilege! Figure that one out, if you can!

If I hadn't known exactly what Mrs. Beatty looked like and precisely where she was sitting, there might have been a different ending to this story. But I did know and, after a frightening moment of indecision, picked her out and asked her to come on-stage. She calmly walked into the cage, cracked her whip, and cozily fraternized with the tawny beasts.

At this point our insurance salesman was wishing he'd sold himself a policy. He was ready to collapse. And it didn't help any when I introduced Mrs. Beatty as a veteran lion trainer. He was stuck and he knew it.

Mr. Beatty herded the lions back out of the cage. We placed a baseball catcher's mask on our contestant's chalk-white face, thrust whip, gun, and chair into his hands, and whisked him into the arena.

"Stage manager," I yelled excitedly, "open the ramp doors and let the big cats in. We're ready to go!"

The audience half rose from their seats in amazement. The contestant steeled himself. The trap door snapped open. And into the cage capered *a dozen jittery alley cats!*

Our most risky stunts are not those *inside* the theatre studios, but the *outside* experiments where a number of uncontrollable factors begin to complicate the situation. We take all reasonable precautions and figure all possible contingencies in advance, but still we never really know what's going to happen because the people the contestant meets and the places he goes are not ours to control.

That's why we carry $100,000 insurance with Lloyd's of London!

Take the time, for instance, when one of our meekest contestants started a riot.

We planned this particular stunt as a test of the reactions of a crowd of diners to a fuss that would occur during the peak of the dinner hour at the popular Melody Lane restaurant, located on the famous corner of Hollywood Boulevard and Vine Street.

One of our volunteers was sent off-stage on a trumped-up errand, while I instructed a second volunteer in his job. He was to go to the Melody Lane wearing an identifying white carnation, sit at the counter, and order a piece of lemon pie. With fingers mentally crossed I told him the idea of the white carnation was so that the waitress would recognize him. When he asked for his check, she'd insist upon paying for it herself. I assured him the waitress was pre-coached and that there was nothing to worry about; his job was merely to note the expressions on the faces of the customers at the counter and to return and make his report to us later in the same show. Then we sent him on his innocent merry way.

As soon as he'd left we brought back into the studio the first volunteer, who had no idea of what had gone before. I explained carefully that *his* job for the night was to go to the Melody Lane and get into an argument with an actor whom we had previously planted there. "You'll know the actor," I fibbed, "because he'll be wearing a white carnation and he'll be eating lemon pie." I instructed him further that he was to adopt a belligerent attitude, pick an argument with the "actor," and end it by grabbing the pie and pushing it into the "actor's" face. Then we sent him toward *his* little destiny.

By this time the audience was giggling nervously in anticipation. It was plain we had no "actor" at the restaurant, only another contestant—and *he* didn't know what was coming. As an afterthought, I informed the audience, truthfully, that the management of the restaurant had no idea of the scheme either.

Our assistant producer, the capable and ingenious Irvin Atkins, trailed along behind the second contestant just to make sure nothing serious would develop and to make sure both men would be back in the studio before we went off the air.

The stunt came within a hair of working out exactly as we'd planned. The second volunteer spotted his man at the counter, detected the white carnation, noted the lemon pie, and quickly started an argument. The innocent victim became highly indignant and argued back. It ended when Number Two grabbed the pie, as we'd instructed, and threw it at Number One. But here our plans went haywire. Number One ducked. He really shouldn't have; it would have made things so much simpler.

The lemon pie went skimming past his ear and splattered all over a still more innocent and surprised third party, a customer whose only mistake had been to enter that restaurant on that particular night. He got sore. He got red-eyed sore. He reached out and grabbed the necktie of the pie thrower. At the same moment the "actor" attacked his midriff. The three of them crashed into a wall, fists flying: The pie thrower, who realized by then that something was amiss beside his aim, howled painfully about it all being a "joke." Number One, the intended target, and Number Three, the actual target, screamed something about "murder." From one corner of the restaurant a sailor joined in. From another came a marine. And the riot was on. It took several policemen to end it.

Well, we paid the damages and did a lot of explaining. And we promised ourselves, "Never, never again!" The Melody Lane to this day carefully surveys all customers who order lemon pie. I don't blame them.

Phineas T. Barnum would have been a whirlwind at the game we play each week. His "One sucker born every minute and five more born to take him" proves a shrewd knowledge of people, a knowledge that would have paid old

P. T. mammoth cash dividends in the field of audience participation.

Although Barnum isn't here to receive his check, I'm grateful to him for a whole string of ideas based on the "one-born-every-minute" observation. We like to prove it on "People Are Funny" as often as good showmanship will allow.

The odd part of it is that the average American knows he's fair game for sharpers; he bends over backward to keep from being fleeced. So he gets gypped from behind!

We proved it by sending a man out on busy Vine Street with twenty-five silver dollars. His instructions simply were to hand a buck to all passers-by. He argued, shouted, and pleaded, but he could give away only three of them during the half hour. People were too suspicious.

We proved it by sending a woman out on the street to sell five-dollar bills for a quarter. She tramped for blocks, using high-pressure sales methods, and didn't get a nibble. People, bending over backward, shrewdly suspected fraud, larceny, and skulduggery. We tried a variety of stunts based on the same idea, and people in New York, St. Louis, Detroit, Fresno, and way places reacted exactly the same. They weren't interested in five-dollar bills for a quarter!

We proved it by sending a contestant, in the guise of a philanthropist, into the Tenderloin district of Los Angeles. Shoddy bums, hungry and broke, wouldn't touch the ten-dollar bills our contestant graciously offered them. The citizens of Skid Row suspected a police trap or a capitalistic swindle. They were too smart to fall for such an obvious gimmick. They wouldn't touch the tenners!

We practically wore out a beautiful set of silver-fox furs, valued at five hundred dollars, before we managed to peddle them for twenty-five bucks! We tried it first in Hollywood, where a male contestant attempted thirty sales unsuccessfully. A year later we tried it again in Hollywood with the same result. We tried it in New York . . . and sold the furs almost immediately. Why? Because the woman who bought them from our sidewalk vendor was weaving home from a cocktail party and would gladly have purchased Grant's Tomb. Had she been entirely sober, chances are she would have called a cop.

Wary game, the average American; yet he falls eagerly into the most obvious trap if it's properly "set."

We bagged the limit the night we sent an "Atom Pill" salesman out to snare a few quarters from the gullible. Here's the way we did it:

We rigged an automobile with a false gasoline tank. The regular tank which supplied fuel to the engine was switched to a hiding place beneath the hood. The second tank, the false one, was placed in the normal position. We instructed our contestant, a vacationing schoolteacher, to fill the phony tank with water in full view of the crowd assembled at Hollywood and Vine. Next he was to drop a white pellet, "made from energy-giving atoms," into the false tank. He was to stir the mixture gently, start his engine, and demonstrate the results.

Alongside his parked auto was a huge sign. It said: "Guaranteed Atom Pills. Run your car a thousand miles for only a quarter. One pill does the job of a hundred gallons of gasoline!"

We were "setting" the trap, you see. And we bagged the limit. Our man sold dozens of plain white aspirin tablets at a quarter apiece. The mob fought for the right to buy them. They jostled and shouted and begged for them.

The big boom in atomic aspirin tablets ended abruptly when an ambulance screeched to a stop, sirens blaring, and out jumped two white-clad interns. They clapped our man in a strait jacket and whisked him back to the program.

A murmur of awakening suspicion ran through the crowd of buyers as the "scientist" dropped from view. Up stepped our Mr. Atkins. "Folks," he began, "you've been taken in by a 'People Are Funny' stunt. Will all persons who paid a quarter for an 'Atom Pill' please step forward and I will gladly refund the money."

Do you think Atkins was mobbed? Not at all. The aspirin buyers were so sheepish they wouldn't publicly admit their gullibility. All but two or three of the dozens who had been hooked vanished into the crowd, "Atom Pills" clutched in hands jammed furiously into pockets.

One of the members of our staff is an ex-newspaperman. He looks with jaundiced eye on people in general. "Can't count on 'em to do anything the way they're supposed to," he moans. We asked him to explain one day.

"Take the average person who reads a newspaper," he began. "He reads something and takes it for complete fact. He doesn't realize that every article is simply the fact as seen by one person—the person that wrote the article. And we all know that every person sees the same thing differently.

"If you put five witnesses to an auto accident on the stand, you get five different versions of that accident. A reporter is human. He reports the news as he sees it. It may not necessarily be exactly the way it happened, only his version of it—"

I cut him short. "Wait a minute. I think I've got an idea," and I looked at my partner, Producer John Guedel.

"Art, are *you* thinking what *I'm* thinking?" he wanted to know. And one of the most unusual and certainly the most violent of all "People Are Funny" stunts was born.

A few weeks after that memorable meeting we went about our regular business of putting on a show. Things were moderately interesting at the moment. I can't recall just what mild stunt I was doing. Folks out front in the studio audience were sitting quietly, half of them thinking of problems far and away from a radio broadcast, I suspect.

There was a stir in the seventh row as a beefy gentleman leaned over to ask the woman in front of him to remove her hat. She muttered something back to him and frowned. The man next to her whispered something in her ear. The man in back of her again leaned over and pointed toward her hat. Again she frowned.

I was conscious of this slightly disturbing drama among the studio audience, but I let it pass without comment.

Suddenly the beefy gentleman leaned over again, snatched the offending bonnet into the air, and slammed it into the astonished woman's lap! A loud bellow accompanied the act. From somewhere in the back came an awed "My God!" Then it happened.

The woman's companion thrust out his chin, swirled around, roared, and grabbed the beefy spectator by the throat. Next I knew the beefy spectator was hurtling through the air. He crashed into the aisle, six feet away.

As if they were soldered together, the woman and her companion catapulted after him. Fists crashed into flesh. Bones crunched. Grunts punctuated cadenzas of ripping cloth. Screams of bystanders pulsated through the electrified air. The woman started an uppercut from the carpet and landed on the beefy gentleman's jaw. Next thing she knew, she was cartwheeling down the aisle from a savage backhand to the kisser. Her companion hacked and punched and kicked. Arms and legs flailed. It was a pip of a battle.

While it was in progress, I yelled for the NBC uniformed police, tried to describe what was happening for the benefit of our startled listeners, and attempted to calm the crowd. My hands were full, believe me.

Well, the police finally showed up, buckety-buckety, and hauled the still scrapping trio out of sight. It was none too soon. A flying wedge of servicemen had materialized and was headed for the fracas. If *they'd* got into it, I probably would be writing this in a cell block, serving a term for inciting a civil uprising. As it is, I'm surprised I'm not writing this in a sanitarium for victims of shattered nerves.

After the departure of the culprits, I devoted a minute and a half to the difficult task of restoring the audience to near normalcy. White faces stared at me from all over the house and heaving chests advertised wholesale breathlessness.

I grabbed a hand microphone and rushed into the audience. "What happened?" I asked a woman in the seat adjoining that of the battling beefy gentleman.

"He'd been drinking!" she shrilled. "I positively smelled alcohol on his breath. He was drunk!"

"What did he say to the woman?" I fired at a man in front of her.

"He tried to pick her up," the fellow stated solemnly. "I'm sure he followed that couple in here just to cause some trouble."

"What did the hat look like?"

"It was a red one with three feathers on it."

"It was a brown one with a big veil."

"I didn't see any feathers on it, but the brim stuck way up in the air!"

I asked dozens of questions about the appearances of the departed trio—ages, color of hair, eyes, clothes, what was said, who hit first, was anyone hurt, and so on. No two answers were alike.

When I felt I'd gleaned the last scrap of available misinformation, I broke into laughter and galloped back on stage. From the wings strolled the beefy gentleman, the woman, and her tattered but grinning companion. All three were stunt people from a motion-picture studio! And all three were about as physically vulnerable as the Empire State Building!

Briefly I explained our purpose in staging the fight. We wanted to see how people would react to sudden, unexpected action, and to see what they'd have to say about it later. I denied the presence of alcohol in any of our special guests.

"Well," I concluded, "people are certainly funny when they give evidence; no two people see the same thing the same way." And I waved a good-natured farewell to the three cave dwellers. As they ambled toward the wings the woman suddenly whirled, threw a strangle hold on the beefy gentleman, and neatly flipped him to the floor. Her companion jumped, feet foremost, on his stomach, and all three were at it again. This wasn't on the schedule.

"Hey, you baboons," I screamed. "Cut it out . . . beat it . . . scram . . . the joke's over."

Then my panic-stricken glance fell on the gnarled face of the ex-newspaperman. There was an evil leer on it. "People?" he murmured. "See what I mean? Don't ever count on 'em. They never do anything the way they're supposed to!"

Animals are funny too. That's the reason we use them as often as possible. But I've learned a hard lesson about animals: Never trust them. Even the most virtuous, guileless kitten can double-cross a radio producer.

Almost invariably our furry "friends" become frightened and forgetful, and their betrayal will be impossible to describe to the listener so long as there are censors.

Remember the time Fred Allen had all that trouble with the nervous eagle? It was tame compared with the troubles I've had with turkeys, rabbits, cows, elephants, skunks, bulls, and crocodiles.

Looking over the list, the elephant might naturally be expected to cause the most trouble. True, his contribution is not to be sniffed at, but actually the turkey raised the most havoc with me.

The broadcast was a pre-Thanksgiving show in which some studio guest was to win the luckless bird for a holiday dinner. The orchestra (we were using one at the time) had launched into the opening number and everybody was beaming and happy. Suddenly the bird took off, leaped into the air, and with a tremendous flapping noise soared up and over the musicians. Bedlam!

The audience whooped while I made a stab for a flying drumstick. The orchestra, still playing, squirmed and dodged. It was only natural for the turkey to lose his sense of modesty in all that fuss. From his aerial position he selected his target and started his bombing run. He scored a direct hit on the drummer. He circled rapidly. The string section dropped out of the arrangement and headed for shelter. The bass player was too late. With each swoop of the hysterical turkey, another section of the orchestra would drop its instruments and run. Finally the only musician left was the Maestro. He crouched under a music stand!

You can imagine what kind of a broadcast this made. The listener must have thought we were all stark, staring crazy. And he was right!

Then there was the time we decided to find out what a bull in a china shop would really do. Awkward persons for generations have been likened to a "bull in a china shop," so we thought it was high time we tested the truth of the metaphor.

Our contestant was a florist from Santa Ana, California. And he seemed quite interested in the "scientific research" upon which we were about to embark. Our bull was a Brahma—the biggest, most vicious-looking beast I've ever seen. Two attendants accompanied him, each bearing long poles to keep him under control. The florist's interest in science waned noticeably upon entrance of the bull. I didn't feel so chirpy myself.

We finally got the bull and the florist on their way to the china shop up the street from the studio. The place was managed by a conservative Englishman and his ultraconservative English wife. When we had arranged the stunt the day before, the wife had earnestly begged her husband to have no part of it. She had predicted all manner of catastrophe and swore he'd live to regret the whole thing. She was a very smart woman.

The gigantic bull didn't knock so much as a teacup on the floor as he daintily picked his way through the aisles. He was the calmest creature in the shop, and the only crockery to suffer damage was a vase that crashed to the floor as an astonished customer raced to the rear exit and safety. The visit, however, was not *completely* uneventful.

Back in the studio, the young florist contestant described what had happened. He ended the report as follows:

"It would have been a perfectly simple and peaceful experiment if only the bull had been housebroken!"

As the crowd roared over this unexpectedly frank speech, the Brahma bull looked up, shook his great head, and, as if on cue, repeated the performance on the purple carpet of the National Broadcasting Company!

That was all for *that* broadcast.

Weather Report:
"Brainstorms in the West"

"WHERE DO YOU GET THOSE BRAINSTORMS THAT WE ENJOY on 'People Are Funny'?" Apparently, like the fate of the Ornithorhynchus, a black cloud of mystery shrouds the origin of those zany antics that float along the air waves each Friday night. But really it's quite simple.

Pick up a newspaper. Open a magazine. Ride on a streetcar. Go to a movie. Read the comics. Listen to the people next door. Look in the mirror. There you are. You're all set to write a screwball audience show. Those are just a few of the places where ideas are yelling to be recognized.

One of our writers picked up a paper and read about an eccentric millionaire who had left one of those wills we've all heard about from time to time—something about certain provisions for the heirs to prove before receiving their inheritance. Zingo! What an idea for the show! That Thursday, when Guedel, myself, and four other equally wild-eyed writers gathered for our twice-weekly meeting, this "legacy" item was tossed up for consideration. We all agreed it was worth a try. For two hours an obvious device was chewed, swallowed, regurgitated, and chewed all over again. This first idea was to pick a contestant, lure him into agreeing to impersonate an attorney, and send him out with a legal-looking "will" to pass off on some fellow on the street. But there we ran into a blind alley. We knew it was a richer gimmick than that. Somewhere a Mother Lode of humor was waiting

20

to be discovered. And so we tore our hair, cursed each other, and blasted each new wild idea to bits before our critical siege guns. Then we struck pay dirt. Observe the results:

A young ex-army flyer, still fresh from outstanding service in the Pacific, sat in his small home with his pretty young wife. It was a Friday; the hour: shortly after six. Out of a job, but dreaming of the future, the young couple planned a quiet evening by themselves. They didn't know that Destiny was sitting with them that night.

A knock rattled the front door. Standing there was a solemn, middle-aged man, hat in one hand and a brief case in the other.

"Are you Lester Blank?"

"Yes."

"You're married to Lois Blank?"

"Yes."

"You've recently been discharged from the service?"

"Yes, two months ago."

"Thank you, sir. I just wanted to be sure you were the right Lester Blank. Perhaps I'd better explain. My name is Fitts, of the law firm of O'Connor, O'Connor, Donnelley, and O'Connor. We are representing the estate of Phineas Blister, of Philadelphia. Do you have an uncle Phineas Blister, of Philadelphia?"

The young pilot thought a second, puzzled. Then told the truth. "No, I'm sorry. I don't know of anyone by that name."

"But you must be the right one. Your name *is* Lester Blank, of seventeen twenty-four Winter Street, Hollywood?"

"That's correct."

"Then I am going to assume that you're the man I'm looking for. Phineas Blister died two weeks ago in Philadelphia. He left a rather large estate and a quite unusual will. You have been left a thousand dollars in that will, that is, if you are definitely the right Lester Blank."

The young husband glanced at his wife. "Ehhh—now that you mention it, I seem to recall the name of Phineas Blister.

Very vaguely, you understand. Come in and let's talk this over."

The attorney from O'Connor, O'Connor, Donnelley, and O'Connor fumbled with his brief case. "I'm sorry, Mr. Blank, but we haven't time. I was instructed by my employers to merely make sure you were alive and living at this address. I was further instructed to bring you back to our offices for a more thorough check—tonight—now, if possible. Perhaps you may receive your thousand dollars immediately, if we are satisfied you're the right man."

Well, what would *you* do in a case like that? You'd accompany the attorney, wouldn't you? Sure. And that's what poor Lester Blank and his pretty wife did.

Still puzzled over the queer situation, Lester, his wife, and the "attorney," at approximately twenty minutes after six that same evening, walked on the stage of Studio D at NBC and squarely into the middle of a "People Are Funny" show.

I'd been anxiously awaiting their arrival and I was prepared. I introduced him to the "attorney," who was, of course, merely one of our contestants, and explained we'd picked his name at random from the city directory. But I assured him that he *was* going to inherit a thousand dollars, if he could fulfill the terms of old Phineas Blister's will. Would he try? He would.

"'In order to prove that money is not his Idol, Lester Blank shall appear on the porch of his home tomorrow, Saturday night, at the hour of eight o'clock,'" I intoned, rustling a legal-looking document. "'At that hour he shall reach into a bag containing two hundred dollars in silver dimes. He shall further take a handful of these silver dimes and throw them to the winds. He shall then take another handful, and another, and another . . . until he shall have no dimes left in the bag. All these shall he throw from his porch at eight o'clock tomorrow night.'"

Lester grinned. "Okay."

"By the way, where did you say you lived?"

"Seventeen twenty-four Winter Street," he replied.

"Good. I wouldn't be surprised if there was a big crowd out in front of your house tomorrow night at eight. Will that be all right with you, if they take all those dimes you're going to throw away?"

"Sure."

"Oh yes. There's a little more here in the will. It says: 'The two hundred dollars naturally will be deducted from the inheritance of one thousand dollars.'"

Lester gulped, but before he could demur, I quickly reminded him there'd still be eight hundred left for him.

There were more than two thousand excited people on Lester Blank's front lawn the next night at eight. Not a few of them were trampled in the melee. A score of policemen directed traffic, treated bruised eyes, and kept a semblance of order. But Lester got rid of his dimes.

The next Friday night he was back at NBC to report on the affair. He admitted there was a terrific mob and that his neighbors were pretty unhappy over their broken shrubs and mashed lawns.

"Uncle Phineas wouldn't want your neighbors to suffer for something you, his nephew, had done," I pointed out. "Better give us another hundred of your inheritance to pay those neighbors for the damage you caused. That leaves you seven hundred. Congratulations."

Rod O'Connor, our announcer, interrupted. "Art, this is really none of my business, but I was looking over the late Blister's will and I think there's still another provision."

"There is? Let me see the will. Oh yes. Mmm . . . Listen, Lester: 'And furthermore, in order to prove he not only does not love money, the aforementioned Lester Blank shall also demonstrate to the satisfaction of the attorneys his business acumen by entertaining in his home all persons with a scheme for making money. And in one week he is to select the quickest, surest method of increasing his capital and shall reward the person submitting that method the sum of one hundred dollars. The sum of one hundred dollars shall, of course, be deducted from the balance of the original inheritance, since he already shall have proved he does not care too much for money.'"

The next seven days saw all manner of schemers, promoters, salesmen, touts, gamblers, beggars, and sharpers visiting the little bungalow on Winter Street. Hollywood is swarming with them. And they swarmed on the Blank house.

On the night of the seventh day, back came Lester to the program. With him came a fellow who had suggested, since Lester played a musical instrument, the band business. The promoter said he booked small bands into night clubs and that if Lester had such a small band, he'd have plenty of work due to the publicity he was receiving on the air. We paid the promoter his hundred dollars.

"Well, Lester, that leaves you six hundred. It's all yours. Congratulations, and thanks for—"

"Art . . . just a moment, please." It was Rod O'Connor again. "You still haven't read all of this will. Better look at it again before you give Mr. Blank that six hundred."

I looked again at the will. Strangely enough, it did have another proviso: "And furthermore, in order to prove his kindheartedness and understanding of those less fortunate than himself, the aforementioned Lester Blank shall, on the succeeding seven nights, take himself to that portion of the city of Los Angeles known as Skid Row. And there he shall approach worthy outcasts who obviously are in need of a helping hand. He shall listen to their stories, dressed in clothing which shall be of the same poor appearance as that of the subjects of his generosity. And he shall weigh those stories, giving a ten-dollar bill to each of the persons he deems fitting. He shall so distribute ten-dollar bills to the amount of two hundred dollars. The two hundred dollars, natch, will be deducted from the balance of the inheritance."

So off went Lester the following seven nights, giving out

ten-dollar bills to all the bums he could find, until the two hundred had vanished.

Back he came to "People Are Funny" with his report. He still had four hundred dollars coming to him, but this time he knew he had small chance of getting it. He was right.

"Gee, Lester, you've been having a tough time earning that thousand dollars old Uncle Phineas left you. But you still have four hundred. So keep it. It's yours."

Again the voice of Rod O'Connor interrupted. "Art," he said slyly, "aren't you forgetting about another uncle? Uncle Sam?"

Of course! Uncle Sam doesn't allow people to go around inheriting a thousand dollars without paying inheritance tax! And inheritance tax is pretty steep, too. Add to that the state inheritance tax. And of course the attorney's fees have to be considered.

"Lester," I moaned, "do you know what all these taxes and fees amount to?"

Lester was beyond answering.

"Well, according to some rapid calculation here, you're stuck for four hundred and fifteen dollars. Holy smoke! That's fifteen more than you inherited in the first place! But you've been a good sport about it all, so . . . we'll forget the attorney's fees. All you have to lose is an even four hundred bucks! . . . Gee! That doesn't leave a cent!"

Lester's jaw dropped to the stage floor. He was a broken-hearted man. The audience frowned, and if somebody had started it, we'd have had a riot on our hands. I imagined listeners from coast to coast, who had been following the affairs of the likable young flyer, were putting pens to paper to tell us off.

"Lester, we played a dirty trick on you. I don't want you to go out of here tonight empty-handed. Here . . . have a package of cigarettes." And with that I sent the poor guy back to his chair and told him to sit down and enjoy the rest of the show.

We carried on with other stunts for the next fifteen minutes. As the clock began to nuzzle the hour for signing off, there was a knock at the door of the studio and a messenger came in. He handed me an envelope. I glanced over it quickly, then began to read it aloud:

"Dear Mr. Linkletter:

"I heard a man on your program a few minutes ago and I think he's the man I've been trying to find. Three nights ago, down on Main Street, a man came up to me and asked if I needed some money. I told him I did and he gave me ten dollars. Then he looked squarely at me and said, 'Good Luck.'

"Well, Mr. Linkletter, I took his advice and put the ten bucks on Good Luck the next day at the races. The horse came in and paid two hundred to one. I'm enclosing my friend's share."

And with that I pulled out a thousand-dollar bill. And I gave it to Lester with the best wishes of the sponsor.

He was an extremely happy contestant.

While reading an adventure magazine, writer-producer John Guedel caught himself wondering what was going to happen to a message set afloat on the ocean in a sealed bottle. The hero's life and the fortunes of his beautiful sweetheart depended on who picked up that bottle. From that second the magazine story remained unread as a "People Are Funny" stunt was conceived. A message in a bottle! With a fortune for someone in it! Surely we could figure out some angles to make this one into a big "continuing" stunt . . . and after a few hours wrestling over our hot typewriters, this now-famous Treasure Hunt was born.

A young, adventurous guest was picked and given a "Course of Instruction" in piloting and aerial bombing. He was seated in a rickety "mock-up" of an airplane and told he must fly from Hollywood to New York in five stops to win a big prize. His jumps from place to place would depend on giving the right answers to five key questions . . . but each "miss" would take him off his imaginary course and into the path of various aerial hazards. Then while the studio audience howled, and the listeners pictured the amusing situation, we bombarded him with legitimate and "trick" questions that had a pseudo-aerial flavor and which got him off his course often enough to run into (1) a hailstorm of chipped ice out of a bucket, (2) a sandstorm blown over him with a powerful fan, (3) a flock of geese dropped from overhead, and (4) a rainstorm shot from five seltzer bottles. All of these penalties for getting off the beam could be easily visualized by the listeners, and the questions were carefully picked for "double-cross" answers.

When he finally qualified as a pilot-bombardier, he was given a beautiful set of silver and told that he was next to be briefed for his most important mission. On the following day he would be flown over the Pacific Ocean in a real plane, twenty-five miles off Catalina Island, and there, at an altitude of five thousand feet, he would bombard the ocean with twelve Plexiglas balls. In each of these carefully sealed inch-thick plastic-walled globules there was placed a small ivory treasure chest. In each chest was a note with a "key" word and the directions for calling or cabling the program in Hollywood. We then announced that the first person to find one of the twelve balls, open it, read the note, get in touch with us, and supply the code word, would get one thousand dollars in cash! Furthermore, for each day that passed for one year in which no ball was found and correctly identified, the contestant would receive one dollar.

The contestant DID drop the plastic globes, but NOT the next day, and NOT directly off Catalina Island. Experience taught us not to underestimate the nerve and resourcefulness of amateur treasure hunters. To prove it once again to ourselves, the producer and I took a joy ride the next day out to the announced site of the "bombardment." Sure enough, a half dozen fast motorboats were prowling the ocean surface waiting for the plane. We made a half dozen trial runs at various spots and laughed to see the boats streaking after us. I wonder if we could have broadcast the comments of the "volunteers" in those boats. . . .

There followed an ocean-wide treasure hunt staggering in its proportions. Wires, letters, and cables came in from Alaska, Australia, the Philippines, Catalina Island, South America, and one writer even sent in a claim from Lake Superior. We convinced him that no Pacific tides high enough to cross the Rocky Mountains had been reported in the last few years!

How many vacationists, seamen, and shore dwellers have searched the shores of the Pacific in vain we have no way of knowing, but here is one letter out of many that brought me a hearty laugh:

DEAR SIR:

People aren't just funny . . . they are CRAZY. I'm an auditor-accountant who took his first day off for a fishing holiday in many a year. I had just begun at Point Lobos about 8 A.M. when I sighted something bobbing up and down in the water about a half mile out. At first I thought it was a boat buoy, and then I thought of your program and the thousand bucks! I figured it would come up on the beach at Carmel, so off I went. I ran the car up as close as I could on the sand, got out, and started the search. First I stood around and tried to see over the breakers. Then I climbed a small tree (tearing the pocket out of my coat on the way up) and looked out over the ocean. Finally I gave up and decided to beat it and get in some fishing. So I got in the car and began to back out, but I had driven into the sand too far, and the more I raced the motor the deeper the back wheels dug, until finally I was really stuck. So I walked to a store, phoned a tow service, and came back to wait. While looking out at the ocean, I thought I saw the ball again, away out, so I walked half a mile to the boat rental place, got a rowboat, and set out for the open sea. Two hours later I still hadn't sighted the damned thing, and by this time I was half a mile offshore, bogged down in a bed of seaweed about a mile wide. My oars stuck in the stuff and the boat would hardly move, but I finally got out, started for shore, and had just about reached it when I saw the ball bobbing up and down against a piling under the pier.

I rowed over and, with a yelp of surprise, picked up a . . . red balloon!

If you expect me to ever hear your show again or buy your sponsor's product, you'll (1) refund me $5 for tow-car service; (2) refund me $1.50 for boat rental; (3) send me a bottle of sunburn oil; (4) arrange for me to get another day off to really fish.

You and your damned treasure hunt!

Disgustedly,
A FORMER LISTENER

After a year had passed, and no one had reported finding one of the floating treasures, we recalled our original "bombardier" and paid him one dollar for each day in the year during which the prize had remained unclaimed: $365!

What happened to the twelve balls no one could even guess. Scientists at the Scripps Oceanography Institute in La Jolla pooh-poohed any chance of them being found, and pointed out that of three thousand messages flung into the Pacific by their research people some years ago, less than five had ever been returned.

We had visions of some ignorant and superstitious native tribe finding one on the shores of a far-distant Pacific isle and setting it up as a new god in their witch doctors' collection.

Then, when everyone had given up the search and we had almost forgotten about the existence of the twelve balls, a wireless message came crackling across the ocean from Commander Miller of the United States Navy stationed in the Kwajalein-Marshall group of islands and atolls. "Native boy, Klenre, of Eller Island has found your plastic ball with code word 'Raven' inside. Is the thousand dollars a gag?"

This was in the summer of 1947, more than a year and a half after they had been dropped off the coast of California. The ball had traveled more than forty-nine hundred miles. Native Boy Klenre had seen it glistening on the shore of his tiny atoll, suspected it was a floating bomb, and taken it to the Navy headquarters for checking. There, under water, it was carefully opened by suspicious intelligence officers. And today "Millionaire" Klenre is the envy of the South Pacific islanders!

That kind of stunt is particularly valuable because of its "carry-over" value. By that I mean sustained interest for weeks and months. Sometimes we work out gags which run for a month at a terrific pace; such as the time when we had two homeless families competing for a four-thousand-dollar, streamlined, aluminum house trailer. A soldier, his wife, and little girl contested against a sailor, wife, and little girl in a quiz test which brought them back to the microphone every week for four weeks. The whole country chose sides for that one. And we were lucky enough to have the final question on the final night be the one which decided who was to win the coveted trailer. Of course, after whipping up that much sympathetic interest for both sides, it was necessary to provide a worth-while consolation prize for the losers. We certainly filled the bill when we came up with a beautiful suite of rooms in the Hollywood Plaza Hotel AND an appeal over the air for a house to rent. Before the week was out more than two hundred telephoned and written offers of homes were received; enough to take care of the losing family and many more ex-servicemen's families.

That brings me to the next category in our analysis of the origin of ideas. Important community needs provide a worth-while and fascinating source of material. Community-chest drives, jobs for veterans, war-bond sales, the fight against the black market, and housing campaigns are just a few of the causes we have dramatized through "People Are Funny" stunts. We've found that a single individual, telling about his own troubles, or kidding about them during a stunt, is more effective than a dozen announcers reciting facts and figures about thousands of suffering people. Southern California has been one of the worst places in the nation in which to rent a room, an apartment, or a house. Immediately following the war, tens of thousands of veterans and their families were desperately seeking places to live around Los Angeles. Like other shows, we had made appeals to home-owners to open up spare rooms or even garages for these homeless folks. Very few responses came our way. Until I went on the air and said that I had made a bet.

I had bet Guedel that I could interview ten different ex-servicemen and find each of them a place to live before we were off the air that very night. Our ten guests, representing every branch of the service, were seated on stage. In back of them we had optimistically built a small telephone exchange with five operators ready to handle incoming calls. A special telephone number had been secured, and I announced this several times during the interviews.

Before I had even found out where the first marine had come from originally, what his rank was, or anything about his family, the switchboard lit up like a Christmas tree with offers of help. As we went on through the show and told of each individual need and ability to pay, the calls kept piling up until we had enough places to care for several hundred families. Those places had been there all the time. The people had to be stirred by a personalized "me-to-you" approach which an interview or a stunt dramatizes to the final degree.

Of course, if a show is to maintain a high degree of popularity, it must be constantly concerned with the things that everyone experiences and talks about. If you want the most fertile spot of all to go looking for ideas, go to the place where most people go most often: the movies. Each week an estimated eighty million Americans forget their worries for a few hours as they sit in picture houses from coast to coast, lost in the excitement, love affairs, and fun of the silver screen. You can be sure that anything which occurs frequently in movies is going to be familiar to everyone in your listening audience.

Familiar indeed is the character who sits behind you chewing peanut brittle and making whispered comments about the picture. We took care of him in the stunt where a man was loaded down with paraphernalia, drenched with water, and sent into a crowded theater to test the courtesy and patience of the customers.

Then there is the absent-minded gal who has lost her gloves or hat or handkerchief or bag and comes back with the usher to look under all the seats just at the time when Clark Gable is kissing his sweetie. We handled this common complaint by stealing a woman contestant's shoe during the first part of a stunt and then telling her she could find it somewhere on the main floor of the Hollywood Pantages Theatre. We gave her a couple of meager clues, a big flashlight, and a house slipper to wear until she located her shoe. What went on in the theater that night shouldn't happen to my creditors!

There is the obvious stunt to be found in the secret ambition of most moviegoers to be a Hollywood star! We capitalized on this in many, many ways. We have flown hopeful candidates from all over the country to the film capital for screen tests of one kind or another. We have had guest stars from pictures teach volunteers how to act. Sonny Tufts one night almost collected a shiner from a husband who thought

Mr. Tufts' technique a little too enthusiastic when he was going through a love scene with the fellow's wife.

Strangely enough, the least successful way of getting new and original ideas is to appeal to the listening audience!

Present-day audience-participation programs have progressed to the point where professional stunt men are necessary to get a new twist to an everyday incident. All the old parlor games and jokes have been used dozens of times, and the fun books have been thumbed through until every standard device has been worn thin. As almost every program has discovered when a contest was conducted, the ideas sent in are shopworn, obvious, or unworkable. Only one letter out of a thousand has something in it that might be used after drastic alterations had been made, and this is not worth the trouble and expense incurred. Let's face it: the business has become a highly specialized, thoroughly involved operation requiring technical skill and the experience necessary to decide what is purely visual fun for a studio audience and what is fun for the viewers at home. You can judge for yourself the degree of proficiency each producer has acquired by listening to any audience show and counting the number of times the master of ceremonies has to *describe* the fun going on, instead of having the fun convey itself to you, the listener, without explanation!

The man who deserves most of the credit for the successful completion of the "outside" stunts on our original show is Irvin Atkins, then an assistant producer, now the show's director. Today's "stunt" man still manages to wear as many hats as Mr. Atkins did. He is the official observer, fixer, "con" man, riot squad, protector, and all-around Houdini. He must whisk the contestant out of NBC into waiting cabs, parades, elephant howdahs, diving helmets, airplanes, and coffins. Then, evading the crowds of waiting "scavengers" who hang around NBC exits waiting to cash in on the night's plunder, he must see to it that the contestant arrives unobtrusively at his destination, whether it be a private home, a library, police headquarters, show girls' dressing rooms, or a roller coaster. Then he must stand at a distance where he will not be noticed or intrude on the stunt and yet be able to hear or see well enough to know when to yell for help, start breaking down the door if they're inside, pay off angry citizens with folding currency, and explain that the pandemonium is "all in fun." Finally, with seconds to spare, he must burn the road back to NBC in order to save my neck by having someone there to report on what happened.

The record is remarkable when you consider that in nineteen years of harebrained stunts none of our assistants ever has failed to have the guest back in time for a report. Only one, Irvin Atkins, returned so late that I had given him up for lost.

We had dressed a man up as a "bum" with battered felt hat, ragged coat, and mussed shirt. We took all of his money away and gave him a genuine thousand-dollar bill to spend. However, he had to spend it on items worth less than twenty-five cents each, and every purchase to be a single one, and in a different place. We were taking no chances on a big "blowout" at our expense. The real purpose of this stunt was to test the reactions of small shopkeepers, soft-drink proprietors, and candy-counter attendants when a tramp walked up, ordered a dime drink, and after sipping part of it laid down a thousand-dollar bill in payment. Strangely, only one clerk doubted the authenticity of the bill. The rest of them got mad, grabbed the unfinished drink or candy or smoke back from our amateur psychologist, and told him to beat it with his "con" game. The one doubter promptly picked up the phone and called the cops, but of course, before the puzzled desk sergeant at headquarters could make out the nature of the complaint, our Mr. Atkins had paid the bill and the two vanished.

The unplanned part of the stunt which almost upset our applecart occurred in a big department store where the thousand-dollar bill was put in a metal container and shot upstairs through a pneumatic tube for checking. Atkins was pulling his hair out by the roots by the time the long, agonizing minutes had ticked off and the correct change came back. And the way the two of them ran out of the place with the change must have given the poor clerk a case of near heart failure. That bill must have been put under a triple magnifying glass inside of two minutes!

My "bum" volunteer arrived in the "People Are Funny" studio with just thirty seconds to blurt out a hurried explanation of what had delayed him.

And then, to show how far strange coincidences can go, the Amos 'n' Andy show which immediately followed us began its story that night with the loss of a thousand-dollar bill by Amos!

Most fertile field of humor in any audience-participation program lies in that ancient institution, marriage. Pit husband against wife and you have the foundation for funny stuff that can't be duplicated any other way.

Ask the husband to describe his wife's hat. It's as simple as that. Ask the wife to describe her husband's proposal. Rich human-interest material as earthy and basic as a loaf of bread. At least half of our stunts are built on this common theme.

The stunt may be simple and brief. The husband is sent to a soundproof booth, the wife to another. The listener and I can hear both of them, but they can't hear each other. I ask each who is boss around their house, who handles the money, who decides important mutual problems, and similar questions. Their divergent answers make the stunt successful as millions of husbands and wives imagine themselves in the same position.

The theme can be developed as extensively as necessary, even to the point of continuing a stunt for two or three weeks.

Out of a hundred such stunts built on the marriage theme, the most illustrative that comes to mind is one we did on the subject of shopping.

It started when a man and wife were selected by the studio audience from among several volunteer couples. Casually I questioned them about marriage and slyly I steered the conversation into channels having to do with trust in each other. The more I needled them, the stronger grew their avowals of implicit faith. Once hooked on that score, I switched the subject to shopping and without difficulty made both of them admit they had full confidence in each other's bargain-hunting talents. It was simple to tie together the general admissions of trust and faith. I clinched my "suck-in" by asking point-blank if the wife would risk her own safety and happiness on her husband's dependability as a shopper. Her indignant "yes" was all I needed. They were in the frying pan.

We unveiled a diabolical machine, a stationary armchair equipped with chains. Suspended over it was a tremendous frosted layer cake. Connected to the shelf holding the cake was an alarm clock. I explained that when the clock rang, the cake would fall squarely on the head of the person strapped in the chair beneath it.

"You said you'd risk your happiness on your husband's dependability," I smiled at the wife. "We'll see. Step into the chair, please."

Quickly I gave the instructions to the husband. He was to purchase a number of household items without benefit of a written list. He was to memorize them as I gave them. He nodded brightly, and I rattled off flypaper, salad oil, library paste, a cot and mop.

The last two items I purposely slurred together. It sounded like "a cotton mop." I wanted it to sound that way, for that was the trap we were setting.

"Now, Mr. Jones, your wife's happiness depends on your memory and on your ability to efficiently procure those items.

If you return in fifteen minutes without all of the items I mentioned, the cake falls. And if you return later than fifteen minutes, the alarm clock rings and she gets it anyway. Okay, get going!" He scuttled for the door, mumbling over and over the items he'd been instructed to obtain.

Fourteen minutes later he returned, parcels carefully held in his arms.

"Did you get everything?" I wanted to know. He said he did. "Swell. How does it feel to be a rescuing hero?" As he answered, we unstrapped the wife and freed her from the chair. Then, as if it were an afterthought, I asked him what he would have done if he had failed in completing his shopping mission. Would he have volunteered to get into the chair and take the penalty in place of his wife?

Since his job was done, he went overboard with his answer. Naturally he'd be willing to substitute for his wife. And he smiled smugly. The audience nodded pleasantly and it looked like the stunt was over.

Suddenly an assistant shouted: "Hey, Art . . . where's the cot and mop?"

"What!" I exclaimed in horror. "No cot and mop! How did this happen, Mr. Jones?"

His tongue went dry as he explained sadly: "I brought a *cotton mop* like I thought you said." His eyes turned to the layer cake. All eyes in the audience followed.

"I'm *so* sorry, Mr. Jones." Yeah, I sure was sorry! "But hearing orders and filling them accurately was the test. And since you have just stated before fifteen million people that you would happily substitute for your wife if you failed . . . well . . . your chair is waiting!"

Our cake-dropping experts never miss. They've had too much experience. Mr. Jones, as target for the day, got the cake.

Easily our most successful man-and-wife stunt involved the use of a phony fortuneteller, a concealed set of headphones, and a co-operative wife. The husband had been sent off-stage on a wild-goose chase while I explained to the audience that upon his return we would introduce a "gypsy" seeress with a crystal ball, and I would challenge him to disprove the existence of her ability to tell about the past, present, and future. Actually, while the man was out of the studio, we had kidnaped his wife from her seat in the audience, taken her to a concealed place backstage, and given her a telephone which was connected with a pair of hidden earphones beneath the elaborate headdress of our fake fortuneteller.

The idea was to have the wife hear the questions and tell the "gypsy," so that apparently she could actually see what happened in her crystal ball. Needless to say, the "gypsy" was one of Hollywood's smartest young actresses, Lurene Tuttle, who could stall with meaningless phrases while the vital information was being given her by the hidden wife of our victim.

In a sense, we had built a super lie-detector. And not the least amazing thing is the wholehearted enthusiasm with which either husband or wife enters into a plot to trick the other one. In fact, sometimes it is almost frightening.

Great care must be exercised lest any serious real-life differences be exposed or stirred up, because the slightest feeling of actual anger or bitterness not only spoils the fun but offends the listener. In rare cases it can even become a matter for court action.

I am told that one program just missed a lawsuit by a quick out-of-court settlement when they tricked the husband into talking about his wife whom he thought to be thousands of miles away on the East Coast. He had been picked without his knowledge from a group of men who had requested tickets to the program several weeks in advance. The rest of the gang were "in" on it, and the man's wife was brought out to Hollywood by plane and disguised with a veil and false wig. Then, on the night of the show, the husband was sent out to have dinner with a starlet to a popular restaurant, and she led the conversation around to a discussion of his wife. The poor fellow was unaware not only of the fact that his wife was sitting in the next booth, but that a hidden microphone was carrying his conversation to the listening audience.

"I'll bet your wife would like to be here with you," the starlet teased.

"I'll say she would!" He laughed. "And am I glad she isn't here. The old bag is about ten years older than I am, and she watches me like a hawk!"

"Oh, I'm sure you're just kidding," the girl protested, embarrassed by the knowledge that both the wife and the nationwide audience were listening.

"Kidding, my eye," the unruffled husband boomed out. "I've been trying to get a separate vacation for ten years, and if I had my way, I'd never go back."

At this point the frantic signaling of the producer had the desired effect, and the engineer cut off what was probably the most disastrous bit of conversational frou-frou ever to go out over a major network.

The closest we ever came to such a debacle was the evening that Sonny Tufts was our guest star. We had chosen a young married couple to be our volunteers, and after the introduction of the Paramount star, I explained that we were going to give the wife a chance to audition for a romantic part in a play that was to be done that very night on the air. We then sent her and Sonny to a rehearsal room off stage to practice, while the husband was to perform another stunt.

As soon as they had gone I told the audience about a hidden microphone in the rehearsal room and asked the husband to join us in eavesdropping on the conversation between his wife and Mr. Tufts.

The studio audience was immediately ready to scream its head off. The anticipation level at this point was at the explosion stage, because they knew that our plot called for a testing of the romantic inclinations of the wife. Sure enough, the very first words spoken by Sonny started the fireworks:

"Before we start, Mrs. Smith, I think I should explain that when we rehearse a scene—for instance, a love scene—we actually try to get the feeling of romance into it by kissing, if the script calls for it."

The next few words were lost in the roar of studio laughter.

"I hope," Sonny was continuing, "that you won't object to this?"

There was a suspenseful pause while the young husband gulped nervously and looked at me.

"Well," the wife giggled a little, "I won't mind if YOU won't."

By the time the loud-speaker could again be heard over the screams, Sonny was asking her if she thought her hus-

band would mind, and when she said that what he didn't know wouldn't hurt him, I thought the audience was going to tear the place to pieces.

The husband proved to be a wonderful sport and refused to become too perturbed even when we brought his wife and Sonny back to the stage and heard her deny that anything more than a prosaic reading of lines had taken place in the rehearsal room.

The extraordinary aftermath of this stunt occurred following the broadcast, when I took the two of them out for a drink to smooth out any possible recriminations, and she told me that as an old "People Are Funny" fan she had guessed there was a hidden microphone in the room and wanted to go along with the gag to make her husband squirm!

Time and time again we are confronted by the eagerness of either husband or wife to double-cross the other, and our only worry is to keep the joke within the bounds of propriety. In the case of the incident I've just related, we received a good many letters reproving us for encouraging infidelity or taking us to task for skirting the perilous brink of a matrimonial fissure too closely.

Perhaps the outstanding instance of a case where one of a married couple was anxious to play a trick on the other occurred in our "Kleptomania" stunt. In this gimmick the wife was told that her job for the night was to test the courtesy of salesgirls at a nearby department store. She was to fuss around, paw over articles, try on gloves, and in every way determine how far a customer could go before the clerk would blow up. After she was gone we brought her husband up from the studio audience and told him that it would be funny if he went up there, pretended he was a detective hired by her wealthy family to watch over her because she was a confirmed kleptomaniac, and had the floorwalker pick her up for shoplifting.

"Funny!" he guffawed. "I'd love to see her face when the store dick goes after her."

"You will," I promised him. "But be sure she doesn't see you or it would spoil everything. Keep behind a pillar or something and be sure to tell them to give her a good scare, because that's the only way her family feels that her urge to shoplift will ever be cured."

"Don't worry," the gleeful spouse reassured me, "when I get through she'll be lucky if they don't throw her right into the brig."

With this we wished him well and sent him on his merry way. As soon as he was out of the studio, I explained that the final scene in the little play about to be enacted at the store might surprise BOTH of them, because while I had been talking to her at the microphone Guedel had been stuffing her purse with costume jewelry, gloves, and other small objects, all freshly purchased at the store to which they had been sent . . . and all of them having the price tag still fastened on!

What we wanted to find out was: Would the husband come to his wife's rescue when he saw the floorwalker actually discover merchandise in the purse? We thought he would.

But when they were finally brought back to the show, separately, and I interviewed the husband at the microphone, he could hardly talk coherently between the happy gasps of laughter that punctuated his story of how she really DID have stolen gloves in her purse and the last he'd seen of her, she was being dragged off to the manager's office.

He was no more concerned than a small boy after a raid on the cooky jar. But all the time he was laughing about the big joke, his wife was standing right in the wings, and when she finally came striding out onto the stage to confront him with her side of the story, I thought that we'd done it at last. She forgot all about the listening audience while she inventoried his various and sundry shortcomings, summing up with:

"Just wait till I get you home tonight. We'll see which people are funny!"

Fun in Bedlam

THE WORLD IS FULL OF FRUSTRATED MASTERS OF CERE-
monies. You find them at Rotary Club luncheons, meetings of
the Women's Auxiliary, Scout meetings, church bazaars, and
at private parties. It looks so easy. All you have to do is
just stand up there and rattle off jokes, introduce people, and
be nonchalant. Anybody can be an M.C.!

Yeah?

It's taken me twenty-six years of hard work. I've died
twenty-six hundred deaths. And some twenty-six thousand
things have gone wrong to make my heart stand still.

Sure it sounds easy when you hear someone gab glibly
for half an hour. Of course it is natural to conclude he's born
with an agile tongue. I don't blame you for thinking that
anyone can be the life of the party.

But let's get a few things straight. Perhaps I'd better
devote a few hundred carefully chosen words to the matter
of "How to Become a Master of Ceremonies."

I've blissfully wandered in and out of more tight spots
with a whole skin than Ulysses and his hapless crew. Everything that could possibly happen to one man on the radio
has happened to me a dozen times. That's why I'm so nonchalant; there's nothing left to worry about!

My first callus came when I was twelve. They were building
the Woodrow Wilson Junior High School in San Diego, California. One day after supper a suppressed desire drew me
to that half-completed building. In the half-light of evening,
in the silence of the eerie shadows, I mounted the stage of
what was to be the huge school auditorium. Striking a lecture-

platform pose, I burst into a speech. I don't recall what I said, but it was my first ad-lib adventure. It had something to do with saving the whole world.

Midway between the starving Armenians and the heathen Chinese a raucous voice bellowed from the wings: "Hey! Get outta here, you brat! Whatcherthink yer doin'?" It was my first critic: he was the night watchman.

Callus Number Two came from a heroic role in a high-school play. It was a murder story and my part was small but, as it turned out, important. The production was the crowning achievement for the dramatic class that year, and fond parents and relatives came from far and wide to be amused and amazed. I don't know how amused they were, but I'll bet my shirt they were plenty amazed.

The plot unfolded according to plan. All the characters were introduced, the scenes set, and the dialogue rolling along nicely. Then Linkletter came on-stage. I was well re-hearsed in my role and I uttered my lines faultlessly. It sounded like a parrot. At least it did to me. I'd been re-hearsed too much, and as I spoke, I felt the whole thing was pretty dull and old. So I began to toss in ad-libs of my own here and there. It sounded a lot better. So I added a few more of my own ideas. I could see the other members of the cast taking a new interest, and I gathered steam. Soon I was thoroughly off the track, inventing an entirely new play as I progressed. Alas! I was the only one who had any idea of what it was about.

The expression of surprise on my leading lady's face changed to horror. There was panic in the prompter's voice as she babbled from the wings. A faint whirring in the distance indicated the author of the piece was thrashing about madly in his tomb.

Well, that thirty-minute play suddenly was condensed to a six-minute vignette with clues, corpses, and detectives scrambled together in the godawfulest mess that ever littered a stage.

Incidentally, another San Diego High School dramatic student appeared in the same play a few years later. He followed the script. He didn't ad-lib. Everybody liked him. Today he's fairly well known. His name is Gregory Peck.

I acquired a number of minor calluses in college, puttering with musical comedies, fraternity affairs, student assemblies, and odd jobs. Most of them appeared on my hands, however, for I worked my way in the college cafeteria. I arrived at the peak of success there when I learned to balance six cups of hot coffee in one hand.

Through my college activities the manager of station KGB, in San Diego, got wind of me and the first thing I knew I was in the radio business as a part time announcer. From then on my calluses came thick and fast. Very thick and very fast.

There was the time I ad-libbed a spot announcement for a used-car dealer. (The original copy had managed to lose itself.) "Folks," I began, "the Don Lee used-car lot has something you've been waiting for. A swell sedan with four doors, new tires, reconditioned engine, and new paint job. You better hurry down today and take a good look, because here's one car that *won't last long!*"

Never content with copy as it was written, I constantly added my own ideas and just as constantly heard from every sponsor on the station.

A black day in the history of broadcasting occurred during my first trying months at KGB: It was the result of my over-developed imagination.

Six of us (four actors, an announcer, and a sound-effects man whose principal source of income came from services as a mechanic in the garage beneath the broadcasting studios) were scheduled to re-create a battle scene as part of a historical series dramatizing World War I. It was to be the Battle of the Marne.

Briefly I'll pass over the battle, and lightly. Suffice it to say that six people dared to reproduce the throaty yells of two divisions of infantry, dared to make cannons roar, dared to bring to life the piercing screams of wounded horses, the moans of wounded soldiers, and all the sound and the fury of a mortal struggle. We six were pretty busy there for a while.

Sitting in the sponsor's booth, breathlessly watching through a sheet of glass twenty-five feet long and six feet high, sat the man who was paying the bill: the sponsor.

I had the all-important responsibility of devising a sound effect that was to climax the whole affair: the sound of an exploding cannon that was to herald the end of the battle scene.

I had borrowed a beer barrel from a neighboring brewery, placed it in the center of the studio and, with the best of intentions, aimed the muzzle of a fully loaded, double-barreled shotgun down its maw. Out from the sound of battle there came my cue, a gasping cry: "The end is here."

Never were truer words spoken. I closed my eyes and pulled both triggers.

The beer barrel flew into ten thousand pieces, each doing a polka as it cleared the rafters. The microphone disappeared into thin air. Far out in the country the transmitter danced a jig and went dead.

There was chaos in the sponsor's booth. There was complete disbelief on the sponsor's face. Twenty-five feet of glass, six feet high, lay shattered in the sponsor's lap. He was the maddest sponsor I ever saw.

Well—almost! there was another one . . .

"Be straightforward, dignified, and, above all, not too cheerful in tone," were the directions which accompanied the commerical copy they handed me one day at KGB. The copy extolled the benefits of an old, reliable, dignified firm of morticians, and the copy was to be read in conjunction with a daily fifteen-minute program of public-service announcements.

Two straightforward, dignified weeks slipped by uneventfully. In fact, to be blunt, it was a pretty dull program. But the sponsor, bless his undertaking bones, was happy.

Until one day . . .

I stood in the main studio, delivering my funeral and funereal announcements. On either side of me was a grand piano, left over from a previous musical program. Suspended from a hook in the ceiling was a cable. And at the end of the cable dangled the microphone.

Attached to the microphone was a steel rod, also suspended from the ceiling. There was a setscrew attached to it for the purpose of allowing the microphone to be raised or lowered to fit the height of the speaker. I didn't know it, but the setscrew wasn't set.

I wasn't too cheerful in tone as I read the announcements, but I proceeded at a neat clip. As I went into some speech concerning the upcoming meeting of the Rebecca Society, the microphone jiggled, swayed, and slowly began to descend. Inch by inch, after the manner of a dying cobra, the mike slid toward the floor.

There was nothing I could do. After the manner of a dying cobra's mate, I accompanied it down.

First I hunched. Then I bent. Then I squatted. Then I kneeled. And finally, as the microphone nuzzled gently against the carpet, I fell prostrate . . . reading frantically about the Rebecca meeting all the while.

All would have been fairly well had Fate not selected that moment to introduce a spectator to the scene. He was a plump, fun-loving musician with a Falstaffian guffaw.

One glance and he was a goner. I will say, in fairness to him, that he did his best to do his laughing silently. He fairly exploded in the effort, but he tried.

At that moment I began to read the commercial part of the program. This was hardly the time to talk about funeral parlors. Somehow it just didn't fit into the way things were going. I just wasn't used to talking about burial plots while lying on my stomach and addressing a microphone. I tittered. I giggled. I strangled a whoop. Then hysteria.

Until that day the sponsor had been famed as a friendly mortician. After two solid minutes of the most amazing funeral commercial in the history of the spoken word, two solid minutes of a duet in wild shrieks, it is understandable that the mortician changed his friendly outlook. He said afterward his commercial sounded like feeding time at the booby hatch! The series was buried and dead.

Counting the calluses? Know why I'm nonchalant now, twenty-six years later? What else can happen? Read on.

Somehow, in spite of the catastrophes that dogged my steps, I managed to become program director of KGB and as such assumed responsibility for other announcers' troubles.

In my days of apprenticeship the rules for operating a local station were far less formal than they are today. In our case we opened the day's broadcasting in the morning by the simple expedient of snapping a switch and talking. At least that was the procedure until a certain morning in June.

Our station opener was a big happy sort of guy with a booming, train-caller type of voice. Promptly at seven each morning he'd open his microphone and bellow: "Hey there! Get outta that bed! It's seven o'clock!" Then he'd begin playing his dance records.

I don't doubt but what his explosive, accusatory opening blast had many repercussions throughout the land. We'll never know about most of them, but we did hear the details of one.

They came in a letter from a man with a cosmic sense of responsibility and a colossal sense of humor. His letter was anonymous, but it had the ring of truth and the outraged tone of a hit-and-run victim.

According to his letter, the young fellow had been married the night before and the bridal couple had departed merrily on a honeymoon trip up the coast. They had driven twenty miles before reaching the understandable decision that that was far enough. So they stopped at a wayside motel near La Jolla.

Like most honeymooners, this couple had spent a rather nervous first night and, after retiring, had turned on a bedside radio for some light, gay dance music.

Somehow, in the confusion of going to sleep, the station had signed off for the night and that fact had escaped our bride and groom. They went into slumber with a quiet but deadly radio set at their side, all hot and ready to sputter.

That was the scene at exactly seven o'clock the next morning. Bride and groom snoring peacefully, sun shining, birds singing; God in His Heaven, all right with the world. Suddenly there issued, in that innocent room, the voice of Leather-Lunged Louie. "Hey you! Get outta that bed! It's seven o'clock!"

Now the groom was new at this sort of game. He awoke with a start, took a quick look around, guiltily leaped from his bed, ricocheted off the night stand, fell to the floor, and fractured his right arm! That was the end of *that* honeymoon. It came dangerously close to being the end of *that* marriage!

The morning following receipt of this letter found a meek little announcer reading the following "opening": "Shhhh . . . Don't be alarmed! . . . It's only me . . . your radio!"

During this period of my radio education I learned to keep my wits about me every moment I was in front of a microphone. Most announcers learn this essential habit during their days of apprenticeship, and I followed the rule. You had to learn or you wouldn't last.

For announcers love to play jokes on each other. When it comes to practical joking, these jolly boys of the radio have no peers.

I've had 'em light fire to my script as I read the stock quotations, throw clawing cats on my back in the middle of a newscast, insert salacious messages into a church announcement, tickle my neck with a feather during a time signal, remove my trousers as I urged listeners to buy a client's bread.

Another common form of humor among announcers is to frighten visitors by reading an announcement, surreptitiously flicking the "off" button, and continuing on without a break to castigate the sponsor, the manager, and the Twelve Apostles. The unenlightened visitor, unaware that the mike has been deadened, is expected to gasp in astonishment and usually does.

But microphones, being run by electricity, are eccentric. The flicking of an "off" button doesn't necessarily guarantee that the microphone will obey the button, and when this happens some announcer may be expected to do the gasping . . . on his knees on the manager's office carpet!

My comeuppance was reserved for a more catastrophic moment than a mere spot announcement on a local station.

I learned to respect a microphone, dead or alive, on July 4, 1935, at the mighty San Diego Exposition.

The exhibit buildings were jammed with curious, perspiring tourists. The roads were choked with pedestrian traffic. The president of the fair was on the stage at the main plaza, and one hundred thousand people throughout the fairgrounds were awaiting the official announcement which would begin the Independence Day program.

This announcement was to come over the public-address system which blanketed the fairgrounds. Great speakers were built into pylons, hung like coconuts in the palm trees, recessed into pavilions, and pointed at every open space where crowds gathered. It was a miniature transcontinental network and it operated from radio headquarters at the fair.

As program director for the big exposition, I naturally reserved the more important announcements for my personal attention, and on this particular day I stood before the microphone, filled with the overpowering significance of my assignment. Picking up the Proclamation, I nodded to the engineer through the glass window, punched the "on" button, and gave it every solemn tone I could muster. Midway through the Proclamation the studio door opened violently and in staggered a particularly poisonous character who had been instructed time and again to stay away. Disregarding my frantic gesticulations, he lurched over to a chair, plumped into it . . . and belched!

Fuming, I finished my pronouncement and punched off the microphone. I stood rooted before it for a moment, glared at my visitor, and then I exploded:

"YOU! You blankety-blank! *If you're not out of the grounds in ten minutes, I'm going to knock your damned head off!*"

All over the fairgrounds plain, old-fashioned hell broke loose. The mike had failed to shut off.

As my words came blasting through hundreds of loud-speakers in every corner of the big exposition, the reaction was phenomenally unanimous: men ran out of restrooms with zippers caught on shirttails; tousled gate-crashers tunneling under fences ripped their trousers to shreds getting back to safety; the president was speechless before a gathering of California Parents and Teachers; and a delegation of policemen, state-guard reserves, and fair officials hurried to my studio. They were not paying a social call.

From that moment I have had a deep and awesome respect for a microphone, whether it be "on" or "off." I treat them all the same now.

It has happened to most of us in the business. Sometimes it is more serious than mine was.

Perhaps many of you will recall a similar experience that took place several years ago on CBS. I was waiting my turn on a coast-to-coast special-event program. It was in connection with the ill-fated French liner *Normandie*. The big ship was on her maiden voyage to America and at the time of the broadcast was somewhere off the coast of France. In New York City the announcer had fanfared the words, "We take you now to the deck of the world's greatest steamship, the *Normandie!*"

I was waiting nervously for the blast of the ship's whistle which was to be my cue to start talking from the Pacific Coast. The short wave crackled and sputtered. Then:

"Colder'n hell out here in the channel today, ain't it, Bill?"

"Yeah, if this isn't the lousiest place for a broadcast I ever saw."

"Wonder who the stinker was that dreamed up this clam-bake . . ."

"Hey, Bill! Who's the guy wavin' that flashlight?"

"Flashlight! My God . . . that's the signal . . . we're on the air!"

At this point there was a dull rumbling sound which might have been the *Normandie* whistle or a man's death rattle. . . . I never did know, because right then my own red light flashed and I was on the air.

Announcers aren't the only ones with pixy humors. Musicians love jokes too. As a matter of fact, studio musicians seem to have included in their talented make-ups a streak of small boy that bubbles over every so often. When it does, look out for buckets of water over doorjambs, electrified chairs, limburger cheese, and thumbtacks.

Speaking of limburger cheese reminds me of the violinist with a San Francisco orchestra who was about to make his debut as a soloist. His pals, wishing him the best of success, stuffed a big dab of limburger under the chin rest of his fiddle, and that warm night, during a lengthy concerto, the poor fiddler was faced, and I mean *faced*, with a pretty bad time. There was nothing he could do about it, so he just played and played and wished he had been trained as a plumber.

Then there's the time Richard Himber brought his band to our station in San Francisco for a coast-to-coast show. Himber's music is always well rehearsed and the musicians well conducted. They're also well schooled in jokes.

On this particular occasion the boys in the band bribed the studio engineer and, after obtaining his co-operation, set all the clocks on the walls ahead three minutes—without the red-headed Himber's knowledge!

Came time for the broadcast (according to the lying clocks), and Himber gave his famous downbeat. The band played the theme in six different keys. One or two of the men even played different songs. Horrified, Himber tapped sharply on his music stand, glared, and gave the downbeat all over again. It was the same tragic story. By this time Himber had

said to hell with the broadcast, his reputation, his sponsor, and the rest of the world. He was fighting mad. He made up his mind that these blankety-blank so-and-sos were going to play this blankety-blank theme right if they had to stay there all night. Again he stopped them and again he gave the down-beat. And again the band kicked it all over the place. It was no use. Himber, his heart shattered, did just what you and I would have done. He sat down in a chair and cried like a baby!

By this time the false three minutes were up and the boys in the band shamefacedly explained to their leader what they'd done. It is reliably reported Himber then swore to give up the music business and buy a white-leghorn-chicken ranch.

Getting back to announcers (my favorites when it comes to horseplay), let me cite one more common type of studio joke. Every new man may expect it to happen to him sometime in the early course of his training.

This joke is known as "mixing-the-script" joke, and it involves the simple task of putting one page in the wrong place, during the period between the final rehearsal and actual air time. This is what is likely to happen: you are the reader and you're talking away on a newscast. You are about to reach the bottom of a page:

"According to last radio reports, the burning ship was located twenty-eight miles north of Hawaii. The frantic passengers decided the only thing to do was . . ." (You've reached the bottom of the page. You turn to the next one and continue.) ". . . to beat the egg whites thoroughly before adding cream." (Penciled in, you'll find the words, 'Now where in hell are you, Bud?')"

Of course funny things are always happening around a radio studio that aren't on anybody's schedule, including the fun-loving announcers. I suppose funny things happen around a grocery store or a bank or a garage, too. But they lack the dramatic touch that is constantly to be found around a microphone; there is always the danger that the "funny things" may get loose and go out into the listening world. This ever-present danger adds zest to an already exciting life.

One terrible moment has left a permanent scar in my memory. I was busily engaged as master of ceremonies on "People Are Funny." It was the middle of the show and I was working very hard. Of course the studio was full—some four hundred and fifty people. They seemed unusually spirited on this night, ready and willing to laugh at anything. I even caught them laughing when there was nothing to laugh at . . . at least I *thought* there was nothing to laugh at! I realized later that I had been missing something. It was only when Ted Myers, our announcer, handed me a slip of paper with four words written in bright red pencil, that I caught on. The words were: "Your pants are unbuttoned!"

I'll confess I've played a joke or two myself, in times past. I'll never forget the time in San Francisco when I just about sent William Saroyan, the author and playwright, to a sanitarium. Somehow I feel he won't forget it either!

I was conducting a series of celebrity interviews at the time. It was a transcribed series; that is, all my interviews were recorded, edited, and broadcast at a later, more convenient time. Now in case you aren't familiar with a transcription, let me point out that a recorded interview can be censored, changed, shortened, lengthened, and edited much the same as a written interview like the ones in your newspaper. The original recording is "dubbed" or re-recorded on another disk, with undesirable parts eliminated or more desirable parts added.

Well, on this particular day Saroyan and I were sitting in the studio. I was ad-libbing prearranged questions and he was ad-libbing prearranged answers that concerned his well-deserved success as an author and writer of unusual and highly respected plays. The mike was hot, the "On the Air" sign was lighted, the engineer sat in his booth twirling dials, and the interview was progressing nicely.

I had told Saroyan that we were transcribing the interview, that it was being recorded on wax, and that it would be played on the air later that night. But as our interview went along I began to realize that Saroyan thought we were actually on the air all the time! My baser nature, I confess, took over. What an opportunity to scare the pants off a famous literary tough guy! I couldn't let it pass. I didn't!

As the clock moved around and our interview drew to a close, Saroyan settled back to wait for my own closing remarks. They weren't what he was expecting.

"Tell me, Mr. Saroyan," I continued, "is the rumor true that you steal all your plots from the pulp magazines?"

Saroyan blanched and gasped. I went right ahead.

"And they tell me that you yourself spent several months in a sanitarium taking the cure for chronic alcoholism?"

Saroyan turned from pure white to an apple green. His breath was coming in sputters.

"You're quite a gay blade with the ladies, they tell me. And I think you ought to take advantage of this opportunity to squelch all that talk about your being the father of seven illegitimate children in the San Joaquin Valley . . . go right ahead . . . the air is yours!"

Saroyan wasn't in the mood by then for squelching any talk. All he was interested in was getting out of that studio and into the fresh air.

I decided to call it quits before my guest suffered a stroke. So I signed off the program and then I explained that we hadn't been on the air and that my needling at the end would be clipped from the finished product. Saroyan was a good sport, but I must admit his laugh was a shade hollow. I haven't been able to discover if the talented William has appeared before a microphone since that day!

My education as an ad-libbing master of ceremonies was not confined to hugger-mugger in the studios. I was being groomed in dozens of ways. Including the not-so-gentle art of sportscasting.

It was only natural I try my lungs at calling sporting events. I've always been an athlete. I talked the lingo, loved the excitement of competition, and concluded that covering the world of sports with a microphone would be duck soup. I had no idea I was to be the duck.

My first assignment was to cover a rodeo. Any fool knows that a rodeo is a snap to describe: *I* knew.

We will pass rapidly over my first agonizing minutes. All men wearing hats will please remove them out of respect to the body. I died in those first few minutes.

All the color of the West was there; that took a minute and a half to describe. There was fast action . . . but it was too fast and too far between. There were thousands of eager spectators. I took care of them in fifteen seconds. That left me with nothing to talk about. To an announcer that is sheer murder.

I talked some more about the crowd. I talked about the clouds in the sky. I talked about the little yellow dog that always materializes at open-air events. I talked about the state of the Union. I talked about the states of the Union. I talked about unions. I went bone dry.

In desperation, I collared a passing cowboy, hoping *he* could say something. Strong, silent man of the West, that's what he was. All he could say was, "Yep," "Nope," "Uh-huh," and "Huh-uh."

My final feeble gasps quickened suddenly. From the chutes there flew a huge black horse, wild mane sailing, thundering hoofs flashing in the sun, his graceful head arched proudly. It was a magnificent picture. And it was a straw for me. I clutched frantically.

"What a thrilling sight, folks," I shouted, "the high spot of the show so far. A beautiful big horse in a cloud of swirling dust . . . I think it's a mare, . . . no, no . . . it's a stallion . . . bucking, twisting, king of all he surveys. It's the biggest horse I've ever seen, folks. It must weigh—"

Right there I struck a rock. I had no more idea of the weight of any horse than I had of Geronimo's social-security number! A brief, agonizing pause, and I hurtled on:

"Yes, folks, I repeat . . . that horse must weigh at least two or three *tons!*"

That did it. Telephone bells throughout the land summoned an emergency meeting of the American Horse Breeders' Association. Western Union wires purpled as the International Cowpony Club gave the signal for the gathering of the clan. Posses and lynch mobs formed all over rural America. Linkletter's name was mud with tens of thousands of horsemen.

In the mails that followed that tragic broadcast I received lists of weights of all domesticated animals from Adam's Off-ox down through Whirlaway and Seabiscuit, pointing out that half a ton, twelve hundred pounds, was a reasonable heft for a horse. A wire from Ripley urged me to forget the rodeo and interview that biggest of all equine monstrosities!

I had one more tangle with horse lovers. This was the finish. I never will have anything to do with horses again as long as I live. I even snarl at my kids when they ask to ride the merry-go-round.

It was a polo game between San Francisco and San Mateo, played in San Francisco's Golden Gate Park before the largest gathering of its kind in local history. I had been invited to officiate at the public-address system.

To begin with, I know nothing, absolutely nil, about polo. My excursion into the field of describing it was an emergency affair, and I had no time to brief myself on the rules and regulations, customs and traditions, names of players and sundry assorted details with which every announcer should be equipped before he opens his mike.

I took my place before the microphone that afternoon, faced a field as large as the state of Texas, read the starting line-ups as they appeared on the program, watched somebody toss a round white object on the field, and the game was under way.

Back and forth, up and down, sticks flashing in the sunlight, blue blood coursing through their veins, rode these gallant players, walloping the white ball under, around, and across their mounts. As they disappeared into the mists at the far end of the field, I would watch nearby spectators for signs of approval or disapproval. If a sigh went up, I sagely announced a try for a goal had failed; if a cheer resounded, obviously points had been scored. It was easy. I simply selected a likely-looking name from my score card and gave him the credit for the goal.

I thought this to be an eminently fair method, especially since I did not in any way whatsoever discriminate against any of the players; each had his turn at scoring. To keep everybody happy, I occasionally, and in the best traditions of democracy, threw in the name of a substitute. They'd worked hard in practice and I thought it only their due that they receive a nice plug on the public-address system. It would, I thought, give them spirit in case they ever did get into the game.

Somewhere in the early course of the match a stir within the crowd notified me something was amiss on the field. Carefully observing and reporting every move, I noted that the players were pausing in spirited drives down the field to veer toward the grandstand and wave their sticks. This became increasingly regular. I suspected they were angry with the spectators and were urging the crowd to cheer or boo with hotter enthusiasm.

My curiosity was satisfied, however, when in the midst of a chukker every player on the field reined his mount, assembled in a body, and trotted to the grandstand. Right in front of me!

Take it from me, a polo player, blue blood or not, can get just as sore as a stevedore, and both have something in common in their language when they're upset. These were mad polo players. They vociferously demanded: (1) to be given the proper credits or they'd quit the game then and there, and (2) to be allowed the use of my head in place of the regular ball for the next season as a refresher on the rules. That was the end of my polo work.

In the meanwhile I was reaping my ad-lib rewards in radio. I took every opportunity to be assigned to programs that called for extemporaneous talking, whether it was the simple task of announcing name dance bands from popular swing emporiums or acting as master of ceremonies at studio parties. I could see a definite need for such informal entertaining and the demand was growing. I was going to be tops in that field or know the reason why.

Such affairs as the rodeo and polo catastrophes only goaded me into taking on more of the same; I realized that by experience and experience alone could I master the ad-lib technique.

Then the big idea struck: An open-forum program where everybody could have his say!

Remember the story of the innocent friend who stepped in between a battling husband and wife in an effort to bring them back together? Remember his unhappy end?

Such is the fate of the guileless soul who attempts to handle a controversial, open-forum type of broadcast. I was that simple soul. My device was a little package of dynamite called "What Do You Think?" And the idea called for me to introduce a controversial topic of the day and then invite plain, average citizens to discuss it openly with each other for the benefit of the radio audience.

This dandy brainstorm was further accentuated by the red-hot headlines of the day, concerning Lend-Lease, Lindbergh's report on Russia, and Ireland's refusal to open her ports to British shipping.

In short, it appeared that there was plenty of ammunition on hand for some hot arguments. Our only doubt was whether the average citizen would stick out his neck by discussing controversial subjects on the air. We needn't have doubted it. Somebody should have just warned us.

In the rough-and-tumble that was to engulf me in the months to come, I learned every trick of vocal jujitsu. I also looked up the procedure for hara-kiri and went shopping for the knife, before it was all over. It was the toughest assignment I ever had.

We did the broadcasts of "What Do You Think?" from the basement studio of the "Telenews Theatre" on Market Street in San Francisco, and it was broadcast over the West Coast Network of the Mutual Don Lee Broadcasting System twice weekly at 8 P.M.

By the end of the first week the place was jammed to the doors an hour before broadcast time and I would start the meeting a full thirty minutes before going on the air. Thus, by the time I got the nod from the engineer, we had a full-scale battle in full and noisy progress.

Within three months the show was the top-rated Pacific Coast program on the air, and we compared favorably with national nighttime leaders. Conversation in bars, homes, churches, and schools usually got around to "that screwball show where people offered to knock each other's heads off!"

The impossible thing to accomplish in a program of this sort is the position of complete neutrality; the slightest inflection, the least carelessness in the choice of an adjective, and both sides are ready to scream "bias." At one time the FBI had more than three hundred letters from indignant listeners insisting that Mr. Hoover investigate the amount Germany, Japan, Russia, and Great Britain were paying me to put over Communist, Fascist, Nazi, and British propaganda! If I could have played that many parts at once, I would have been sued on the spot by Orson Welles!

One dreadful night the subject of newspapers was introduced, along with their editorial influence on the people of the country. Inevitably the name of William Randolph Hearst was included on the all-round castigating that was going on, and a wild-eyed Hearst-hater started spouting his rancor into the microphone. I realized the spot he was getting me into, but at the same time he was within his rights so long as he did not step into the field of libel, swear, or otherwise violate the laws of the land pertaining to free speech and the operation of a radio station. Well, after a charge that Mr. Hearst was accepting bribes from the German Government, I shut him off and promptly offered the air to anyone who wished to pick up the cudgels for the opposite side.

There was a terrible, chilling silence. It didn't take long to sink in that either by chance or because everyone was worked up to a "hate-the-editor" mood there were to be no defenders of the Hearst editorial policies. Obviously, as a moderator, I could not take sides, so I concluded the argument by stating that since there was no speaker for the defense of the publisher that night, his supporters were invited to attend the next broadcast, would be given an equal length of time for their defense, and could say what they chose. What else could I do? I've asked myself that a hundred times since and still have found no alternative.

But the harm had been done.

A friend of Mr. Hearst's telephoned him a fevered account of the broadcast. Newspaper editors demanded a transcript of the program. And then came the edict from San Simeon: no more mentions of Linkletter or any of his programs in any Hearst paper or any Hearst-controlled radio column!

Despite my protestations of innocence, and the generous allotment of time in ensuing programs to the defense of Mr. Hearst, the order remained in force. And only in recent years has the ban been lifted.

But the daring young man and his flying microphone needed one more lesson before being finally and definitely convinced of the dangers of this kind of show.

I had moved to Hollywood for my first try at the Big Time. Using this series as a springboard, I hoped to get a national sponsor and crash the golden circle of network stars.

My sponsor, the Roma Wine Company, was already becoming skitterish because of mounting war talk, the passing of Lend-Lease, and the "stab-in-the-back" speech of President Roosevelt. Italy had long since ceased to be a friendly country, and a sponsor whose very name was synonymous with the capital of Mussolini's empire had good reason to worry about its "neutrality" in all discussions concerning international politics. It was an unfortunate situation for the Roma people.

In the face of these storm warnings, I gaily moved bag, baggage, and open microphone to southern California, where crackpots, religious nuts, pension planners, and radical zealots of all sizes and tastes assemble to worship the sun and an easy life.

They flocked to our studio like fleas to a hound, and sat drooling in anticipation of me and my pretty little microphone.

In fifteen dynamite-laden minutes these free speakers freely proposed that we: (1) declare war on Russia, (2) annihilate Japan, (3) denounce Great Britain, (4) kill every living German, (5) impeach President Roosevelt, (6) provide a fifty-dollar-a-week salary for every person over fifty years of age. We ran out of time about then, fortunately; we still had hundreds left who had something to say!

Now I don't want to put myself behind another eight ball by intimating that southern California is made up totally of mental whirling dervishes. Obviously the percentage of dimwits hollering from cracker barrels is actually very small. The hospitable environment and salubrious climate of the place attracts all sorts of people, and inevitably the Chamber of Commerce propaganda lures a number of deficients.

At any rate, I was committed to the course, and in full view of the rocky shores that by now loomed dead ahead, I gave the ship her full head of steam. Network executives gloomily shook their heads and Roma Wine Company officials kept the telephone hot with warnings. Then came time for the second broadcast from Hollywood. The subject I'd selected was: "What Do You Think of Hitler?"

Volunteer speaker Number One, a truck driver, sounded as if I'd written his speech myself, it was so sound and free of criticism. "An out-and-out madman," he emphasized. "He's a jerk from the sticks who's got a lotta other jerks hypnotized and I think we should hire a mug to rub him out before this country gets into it."

Volunteer speaker Number Two raised his hand. He was a mild-mannered little guy who sat behind the truck driver. I figured him to be a milquetoast who would give a nice, comfy little criticism of Adolf. He looked very solemn as he made his statement: "I've been giving this matter a lot of thought and study, Mr. Linkletter." I nodded encouragingly. "My considered opinion is that Adolf Hitler is the greatest person ever to live on this earth, including Jesus Christ!"

It was like the calm in the dead center of a hurricane; the pause between the time the fuse has sputtered into the cannon cracker and the explosion; it was the first dropping of the Atomic Bomb!

The War had come to Linkletter. Some people cheered. Some people booed. Some jumped up in their seats. All over, fists waved violently. The truck driver turned around and grabbed the little guy by the necktie. I grabbed his arm before the blow fell and turned to look at the control room. The engineer had a blank, frozen stare like a man who had just seen Beelzebub. The producer held both hands to his head and moaned.

As I held the truck driver away from the little man who had started it all, I jabbered fast and furiously into my microphone over the top of the shouting, noisy din. I reminded the audience of freedom of speech, of United States neutrality, of everyone's right to say what he wanted, how good Roma sauterne could be with ice and soda water, and for God's sake to keep still, everybody, so we could go on with the show. It was no use.

The next morning the least brash young master of ceremonies in Hollywood was available for new sponsorship.

Heigh-Ho! Come to the Fairs!

CLYDE VANDEBURG IS A BIG, GRINNING EX-RANCH HAND, A product of the hills of Colorado. His calm, easygoing manner conceals a keen mind and a driving ambition that has taken him to the very top of the heap in public relations. I accompanied him along a fabulous part of the road to success and count the time among the most interesting and profitable years of my life.

He had only recently resigned a job with the San Diego Chamber of Commerce to handle publicity and promotion for that city's World's Fair of 1935, when I first met him.

"Link," he proposed with no more guile than an Arabian fakir, "why don't you quit your job with KGB and join me?"

Mine was a good job at KGB, safe, secure, and steady. His offer had no guarantees, no security, no future . . . so I took it. And thus I entered a fantastic world of carnivals, wild men, beauty queens, baby shows, presidents, kings, hog callers, cowboys, Indians, and Sally Rand: the unbelievably screwy world of fairs and expositions.

The next few years were to find me first at the San Diego Fair, then at the Texas Centennial in Dallas and the Fort Worth celebration as consultant with Billy Rose, and finally at San Francisco's famous Treasure Island.

While a transient on this fabulous highroad, I acquired one (1) wife, two (2) children, and a thousand and one (1001) hair-raising adventures before microphones, audiences, and footlights.

Since every fair has to have an opening, that was the first assignment handed us at the San Diego show in 1935. Vandeburg and Linkletter were expected to prepare an opening that would eclipse anything in history, and especially the successful and spectacular opening that had launched the Chicago Fair the previous year. It was quite an order, expecting us to eclipse THAT opening. For the nabobs of Chicago had called upon Arcturus, a new star whose light had been heading earthward for millions of years, to make its first appearance to earthly observers at precisely the moment the Chicago Fair opened its gates. As a matter of fact, the first rays from that obscure star were to do the actual opening!

I hope I'm hanging around the Pearly Gates when the president of the Chicago Fair explains that opening to St. Peter and the Angel in Charge of the Firmament. *There'll* be some fancy ad-libbing, believe me!

At any rate, Vandeburg and Linkletter went to work. And what we came up with will eventually call for some equally fancy improvisation. I only hope our explanation to St. Peter about that San Diego opening will be as good as the Chicago president's!

San Diego is the birthplace of the lovely and celebrated California missions. Father Junípero Serra founded San Diego de Alcala in 1769, then progressed northward to San Francisco, founding missions en route.

It was natural, then, that the opening of San Diego's Fair should be associated with the history of the missions. That's why we decided to open the fair by once more pealing the first mission bell to ever call the Indians to worship nearly two hundred years before.

The Fair Fathers okayed the plan, tons of press copy went to the four corners of the land, radio commentators spread the word, and the opening was ready. It seemed as if the whole world awaited the romantic and ancient notes of that historic bell.

As the governor arrived with his staff and hundreds of

thousands of citizens began to gather on the fairgrounds, as the engineers of a nation-wide network began to install their equipment, as the mighty moment actually hove into sight, a small cloud (the one "no larger than a man's hand" rented out to novelists) appeared on the horizon. The caretakers of the mission had finally brought me the bell.

One glance told me it would never stand a baby's tap. Corroded, worn, delicate, cracked, it was indeed a relic, and I knew its mellow tones belonged to the past; it could never ring again without exploding into minute and ancient fragments. It just wouldn't do. It would sound like a garbage can hitting the sidewalk at 5 A.M.

While my conscience conveniently cringed, then looked the other way, I swiped the "C" chime from the drummer of Stan Hite's Red-Hot Dansamaniac's Band. And as an awed and reverent nation, ears glued to receivers in every city and hamlet in America, closed its eyes and imagined itself at Fra Serra's side, there echoed a soft, lovely musical note. The San Diego World's Fair was officially open.

I would like to say, in my defense, that when I whacked that drummer's chime on that festive occasion I sincerely tried to keep in the spirit of the thing: I adopted a cadence I felt sure would meet the approval of the original Mission Fathers!

The substitute mission bell wasn't the only remarkable event attending the opening of that fair. A few minutes after the ersatz peals had echoed across America, an apprentice electrician pulled what is probably the worst boner in the history of broadcasting: He clipped into confetti a maze of wires, nerve center of an interwoven network of fifteen different origination points throughout the fairgrounds! Hell was a-poppin' in no time.

The late Gary Breckner, veteran special-events man, had been stationed high atop a tower overlooking the entire exposition.

He was to co-ordinate the program, giving the cues that

would switch the broadcast to different spots throughout the fair where announcers were stationed, prepared to describe what was taking place at their individual points of vantage.

When the apprentice electrician clipped those wires, he left Breckner stranded high and dry with no communications and a very useless microphone. And he left announcers stranded all over the place with useless scripts and orders but with still live mikes.

After striking the opening notes of the fair on the drummer's "C" chime, I had madly dashed to my own station in the International Village. There, on a balcony overlooking the Spanish Fiesta Restaurant, I was to await my cue from Breckner, then introduce a rhumba band. Those were all the instructions I had. They were all anybody had.

Imagine, then, my panic on discovering that our complicated scheme had disintegrated. There was nothing left to do but attempt to salvage what we could. I assumed Breckner's role.

My first decision was to introduce some Latin music in order to give myself time to check the extent of the damage. I ad-libbed a quick preface to a rhumba and grabbed the intercommunicating party-line telephone. What a mess. Every announcer in all fifteen stations was on that telephone, each yammering for orders.

By the time I realized the futility of putting in my own two cents' worth, the rhumba band had concluded its selection and I was back on the microphone with the success of the whole coast-to-coast show at stake.

Hoping it would work, I took a shot in the dark: "Ladies and gentlemen, we take you now to Gold Gulch, where Bill Goodwin is waiting to give you a shot-by-shot description of the Wild West being lived again in the Forty-niner Saloon. Take it, Bill!"

There was a brief lull. I prayed good old Bill had heard his cue. Then:

"This is Bill Goodwin, folks, standing in the midst of a

scene right out of the last century. Everywhere the rough-and-ready garb of the prospector and cowboy can be seen, with the roar of six-guns punctuating the conversation. Everybody's wearing a beard down here in Gold Gulch and everybody rides a horse. It's the old Wild West all over again. Here comes a Gold Gulch buckaroo now, twirling a pistol loaded with blanks. Hi, pardner! How about giving us a coupla bangs on that pistol?"

Bang!

Silence!

The gun-toting buckaroo had shot his pistol right into the microphone and that was the end of Two-Gun Goodwin's part of the broadcast. It was also the end of that microphone. I took over again, thinking wildly of the next logical place to switch the show. The Organ Pavilion. Nothing could possibly happen there, and I could catch my breath and try to reorganize this nightmare. So I switched to the Organ Pavilion.

Little did I know that the rival NBC had selected that very spot for its own portable transmitter. Somehow its lines had become tangled with those of CBS, over which our own show was going. And instead of my announcer at the Organ Pavilion, I was stupefied to hear the NBC broadcast!

Now things were bad enough. But they got worse. NBC was having trouble too. As NBC's program went over CBS, this is what I heard and couldn't believe:

"This is John Swallow, turning the microphone over to NBC's Ken Carpenter, who is standing by at the Fun Zone. Take it away, Ken!"

There was a second of silence, then, out over the national network of CBS, there came a nervous, thin little voice: "This is the NBC engineer, Mr. Swallow. Mr. Carpenter hasn't showed up here yet. Do you think I could do anything?"

The human mind can stand just so much, then it gives up. Mine gave up right there. Mercifully, everything went black. I suppose we finished that broadcast, but I don't know how or what happened. I only know that I uttered sounds. It was a Tower of Babel.

I had been in the radio end of a World's Fair only one day and already I was an old, old man.

Because I was Radio Program Director of the San Diego Exposition, it fell to my lot to become involved in another nightmare. It happened only a few days after the opening disaster.

San Diego dollars were sponsoring the fair because San Diego businessmen wanted to publicize their city. And they requested that every possible means of telling the nation of San Diego's virtues be exercised. Radio, the most efficient means of reaching the most people with a message, was the keystone of this San Diego publicity campaign and we fair officials were encouraged to originate as many national broadcasts as we could.

So when the Pacific Fleet decided to quit roving around the ocean and come home to its San Diego base, we rigged a broadcast in order to tell the world about it.

The Navy had guaranteed that the mighty fleet would steam into San Diego Harbor at 11 A.M. Two hours before that appointed hour I was stationed at the end of the Municipal Pier, along with thousands of women and children who eagerly awaited the return of their seagoing husbands and fathers. In my hand, as I awaited the signal to start the broadcast, was a list of the ships as they would parade down the bay, with pertinent color material about the fleet supplied by Naval Public Relations. I was prepared to give the nation a thrilling picture of this mighty spectacle.

That same cloud that had appeared on the horizon to mar the affair of the mission bell was back again. Only this time it was larger than a man's hand. Much larger. Large enough to blanket the entire bay. It was a cloud of fog.

Ten o'clock. The fog began to settle. Ten-fifteen. The fog was thick enough to slice. Ten-thirty. A messenger brought news from the admiral of the fleet, advising that he would not risk the ships of his command until the fog had lifted. Ten forty-five. No fleet. Nothing but fog. Should we cancel the broadcast? Not if we were to live in peace with the businessmen sponsors of the fair! Should we postpone it until the sun came out? You can't do that with a nation-wide broadcast; your time comes and you go on the air.

At five minutes to eleven a frantic conference resulted in a reckless and harebrained plot: We would describe the entrance of the United States Pacific Fleet if the fleet was there or not! And that's what we did!

Using the prepared lists, names, sizes, types, and assorted side-light material the Navy had thoughtfully provided, coupled with our own assorted youthful imaginations, we went right ahead with the show. We described the entrance of the fleet!

A few miles offshore cruised the fleet itself, back and forth in the fog. On the deck of the flagship a horrified admiral banged his fists and cursed. Newspaper photographers, newsreel cameramen, reporters, magazine writers, and rival networks tore their hair. It was fraud, plain as day.

Perhaps the most amazing part of that wholesale hoax is that this is the first time, to my knowledge, that any but a few persons ever knew what we had done. Even the CBS brass hats in New York didn't learn the truth until years later.

Certainly the Navy wasn't going to scream that a little fog had deterred its mightiest warships. So the Navy kept quiet. And the newsreels, photographers, and reporters were sheepish too, although they'd been scooped by three hours. So they kept quiet.

You can believe those of us who were responsible for it kept quiet also. Terribly quiet. After all, if "All's fair in love and war," why isn't it logical to assume that "All's fair in love and war *and fairs?*"

I learned plenty during my hitch at the San Diego Exposition, what with strange emergencies popping up almost daily, emergencies that required imagination and wit to meet and solve. It was invaluable experience.

When the San Diego Fair slowed down to a walk, Vandeburg and I charted our course for Texas and the 1936 Centennial at Dallas. Bob Coleson, a new buddy, came along on our new adventure.

Our first job at Dallas, naturally, was to figure out a new and spectacular method of focusing attention on the opening ceremonies. Hold onto your hats; here we go again.

Through the co-operation of the various wireless systems of the world, we planned to open the fair gates by means of a message which would be sent around the world from INSIDE the fairgrounds and which would arrive, after its globe-girdling race, on the OUTSIDE of the exposition. The chatter of the telegraphic instrument receiving this message would activate a mechanism which would, in turn, cause a ribbon to be snipped, officially opening the centennial.

The message was "Texas Welcomes the World." The previous world record for this kind of stunt was something around a minute. We decided that for purposes of a sensational record-breaking stunt, OUR message should circumscribe the world in thirty seconds!

I'll never forget how long that thirty seconds seemed to me, hanging onto a microphone which, in turn, was hooked up to a hundred and fifty NBC stations. I had described the start of the message and then, as a metronome ticked off each dreadful second, I was picturing for our listeners the feverish activity along the route of the wireless highway which those four words were traveling.

New York! Then across the Atlantic to London, where operators waited to relay it to the Continent . . . Russia . . . the Far East . . . a final leap across the Pacific . . . and then halfway across the United States to Dallas and the fair.

Oh, it made a fine story . . . but the message never came back in thirty seconds. Or forty seconds. Or a minute!

In fact, I'll never know if it ever came back. Possibly, in some remote village near Utsk, Siberia, a bearded old operator is still puzzling out the strange syllables of that cryptic sentence: "Texas Welcomes the World."

After forty seconds had plodded by, I nodded a surreptitious signal to a waiting engineer who pressed an emergency button releasing the cutting instrument and the fair was opened!

My job was done at the main gate, so I transferred controls to the main studio, where several top-ranking officials were waiting to make their speeches, and raced for the Cotton Bowl.

There in the broadcast booth built for football games Ted

Husing was waiting to describe the pageant on the field below. I was there to assist him in any way possible.

Of course nothing much happened: the United States Marine Band from Washington got lost, that's all!

Yep. The whole darned band which had been brought at great expense to the government from Washington, D.C., and which was to play the "theme" music for the pageant, had lost itself in the city of Dallas!

An excited official along the line of march, seeing a traffic jam forming up ahead in the parade, decided to get the Marine Band to the fairgrounds on time by taking a short cut, so he waved them off the main street into a diagonal. Away they marched, drums beating, horns blowing, flags flying, to be lost in the suburbs for the next hour!

Husing was terrific. Nothing daunted, he ad-libbed his way through stage waits, confused pageant units, and mistakes. The careless speech that characterized his conversation when off the air was completely gone, and I watched, openmouthed, at the adroit skill with which he marshaled words before the microphone. Skipping back and forth from prepared notes to impromptu remarks, he wove a tapestry of words that hung before me as a goal for years.

In the meantime I was approaching the maddest hour of my life: the opening-night broadcast from the Texas Centennial.

This was to be the climax to end all climaxes. The Judgment Day would surely offer no more spectacular extravaganza.

To signal the turning on of the lights of the fair, we arranged to have a star fall out of the sky right into the exposition!

Actually, a Lone Star of Texas was to blaze its way across the canopy of the heavens and then arc downward to explode in an inferno of light that would spread throughout the palaces and avenues of the centennial as the millions of indirect-lighting filaments blazed on for the first time.

I'll never forget the opening of that broadcast.

I was standing in the central square surrounded by scores of thousands of curious spectators. No one knew the details of the opening, except that a star was to fall from the sky.

At precisely eight-thirty my NBC microphone switched on, and in a low, hushed voice, shielded from the crowd by assistants, I began to explain to the nation-wide listening audience exactly what was to happen.

"Ladies and gentlemen," I began in a tone loaded with meaning, "unknown to the milling spectators who are standing in the darkness around me, there is a plane gliding toward Dallas, thousands of feet high in the sky. All lights are out, and its soundless approach gives no warning. At the controls sits a daredevil pilot whose watch is synchronized with mine. In precisely fifteen seconds from now he will be directly overhead. He will then press a button electrically firing a rocket attached to his wing tip. Then, diving toward the heart of the fairgrounds, with a tail of fire streaming out behind him, he will hurtle downward until only hundreds of feet above us. As his rocket goes out and he swoops back up in the darkness a billion-candle-power star will light up on the roof of the Ford Building, signaling the engineers to throw the main switches and illuminate the fairgrounds."

At this point my sweep-second hand was approaching the zero moment . . . and I looked up for the flash of light which would tell me that the rocket was ignited and the dive begun.

Ah! There it was! Directly above us a pin point of light began to flare . . . and I was off and away in full voice while the crowd around me began to listen excitedly to my gripping description, which was now blaring from the loudspeakers of the public-address system.

Unfortunately something had gone awry on the plane!

The rocket flashed on for a hundredth of a second, then fizzed out for good, leaving the bewildered pilot no choice but to change his course and zoom back to the airport.

But I couldn't change my course. There was no emergency landing field for the verbal flight I had embarked upon.

The listening audience had already been told of our plans. The momentary spark of light had launched me into the epic event and I was irretraceably on my way.

Hoping, praying, trusting that somehow the rocket would flash back on, I kept up my running commentary.

"Closer and closer the blazing meteor is falling to the fair! Its fiery tail streaming out for hundreds of yards behind it, the star is the most frightening spectacle I have ever witnessed."

And now the crowd was beginning to murmur and back away from me. They had looked up, around, and sideways and could see nothing. Obviously here was a broadcaster suddenly gone mad.

Surely the engineers atop the Ford Building would have seen that same flash, waited for it to reappear, and then decide to explode the thousands of flash bulbs that made up the star.

But no! Still no saving flash of light.

I could wait no longer. Even my dim memory of physics left me no choice: an airplane could not indefinitely prolong its dive earthward! So, taking one last long breath, I took the plunge.

"There!—bursting into a billion-candle-power of light—is the most tremendous flash of light in the history of the world! Women and children are screaming with terror! Every bush, tree, and blade of grass is revealed in terrifying detail as the star apparently explodes within the grounds! Folks, this is the most sensational spectacle ever seen!"

I paused for breath.

And in that fatal instant a skeptical Dixie drawl broke the silence at the microphone.

"That man's suah crazy. Ah don't see nothing!"

That's all, brother.

I switched controls and ran for the studio.

If I thought I was to find peace there, I was rudely mistaken. One of the original Texas Rangers had been dug up (and I use the word advisedly) for the broadcast. He was about ninety-five and had been one of the early Indian fighters. With the use of two pairs of bifocals, a powerful magnifying glass, and a script which had been typed in capital letters twice the ordinary size, he was barely able to make out what had been written for him to say. He was in the midst of a lurid description of a massacre when suddenly every light in the studio went out. The engineers had finally thrown the switch for the main lighting of the exposition and blown out all the fuses at the radio station!

Producers, directors, and engineers were running helter-skelter for candles, for flashlights, and in the midst of the pandemonium there stood the old ranger as calm as an August afternoon in the Panhandle, going right on with the story by the light of a tremendous cigar lighter he had whipped out of his pocket. The old boy was still meeting emergencies with a calm hand.

By the time the lights went on and the Ranger had finished his story, a new crisis was developing in the next studio where the program was to be switched within three minutes. A famed soprano who had flown to Dallas from the Chicago Opera Company, and who was scheduled to sing with the official exhibition orchestra, suddenly announced, "I can't sing without my raw egg! Where is my raw egg?" Poor Bob Coleson, who was directing that portion of the show, tried not to look as startled as I knew he felt. He mumbled, "Oh yes, of course, the raw egg. What was it you use it for?"

"Don't be stupid," she flung back indignantly. "My throat muscles will never relax until a raw egg has been swallowed just before broadcast time." She stamped her foot with a fine show of artistic temperament as a page boy darted out the side door on the hunt for a raw egg. He must have found an old hen somewhere, because twenty seconds before the orchestra played the introduction the pullet provender was produced and broken into a cup. It did the trick and the diva sang.

No story of the Texas Fair would be complete without this little gem snatched from the quivering files of the music department. Like most other branches of the fair, this department was more concerned with quantity than quality and so had been decided to produce the biggest singing ensemble in the history of the world.

For two years prior to the opening of the centennial, every school in Texas worked with a set of records which had been made under the direction of the music superintendent for the state. Class by class in school by school, the finest singers were screened from the regular student bodies. They all learned the same pieces in the same key to the same tempo, because the records were all identical. Thus, on the morning of June 20, we were ready to present a chorus of fifty thousand school children singing from the Cotton Bowl over a coast-to-coast network of NBC.

They began to arrive at the fairgrounds as early as eight o'clock. Shepherded by harassed teachers, each little group of excited school kids rushed from building to building, seeing the wonders of the big show. Many of them went breakfastless, some had never been to a big city before, most had never been away from home. At ten o'clock, when they started filing into the huge Cotton Bowl, they were a restless, high-strung bunch of teenagers. Added to that there was the small matter of the temperature. At eight o'clock that morning it was approximately 85 degrees and by ten-thirty the temperature was above 100.

Inside the big bowl a blanket of moist heat seemed to settle down over everything and everybody. Up on the big improvised stage at one end of the bowl my assistants and I were doing everything possible to help the NBC people have a good program. Tremendous parabola microphones had been set up to catch the full volume of the mighty chorus. Twin pianists were waiting to sound the chords which would provide the proper key for every song. The superintendent of music herself was waiting to lead the children. She was a short, plump person who, under the double stress of the occasion and the humidity, was beginning to melt like an ice-cream cone. Everywhere she scurried across the wooden planks a warm spray of perspiration followed in her wake.

Then we discovered an elemental acoustical fact: due to the slowness with which sound travels, every section throughout the stadium was heard at the microphones at a slightly different time, so that those immediately in front of the stage would be heard singing a word, and then those to the side and back two or three hundred yards would be heard singing that same word a fifth of a second later, while the response of those at the far end of the stadium would come booming in a half second after that. It was like four or five echoes coming from the same mountainside.

By the time we went on the air the first omens of what was to come were beginning to be evidenced. Here and there throughout the crowd the smaller children were keeling over unconscious from heat exhaustion. Like an epidemic, sunstroke ran through the crowd, while terrified teachers hustled their small charges toward the nearest exit and shade.

By ten minutes past eleven more than two hundred children were piled under the main platform and the announcer handling the program had a complexion closely resembling the underbelly of a shark. One look from his glazed eyeballs and I began to edge toward the front of the stage for the inevitable collapse. Sure enough, five minutes later he staggered to the side and I took over. After all, what could the sun do to me? I was already out of my head.

Discarding the script, I began to talk to the kids just as if we were not on the air but, instead, assembled for a big picnic. I instructed the ushers to assist the teachers in getting their small ones out through the exits and rallied the larger kids into a crowd of some two thousand voices directly on the floor of the stadium before the microphones. Then, with this considerably diminished choral group (we had dropped from fifty thousand to two thousand in twenty minutes), we finished the program somehow without panic. The rest of the day was pretty much a madhouse. Lost children, lost parents, and lost teachers cluttered up the waiting rooms, police sub-stations, and exhibit palaces. The music department certainly had accomplished one purpose: it produced the most gigantic clambake in history. I know—I was there.

SAN FRANCISCO WORLD FAIR NEEDS RADIO DIRECTOR. IF YOU ARE STILL AS CRAZY AS I THINK YOU ARE YOU WILL TAKE THE JOB. AS EVER. VANDEBURG.

This provocative wire arrived just as the Texas Fair was folding its tents and the Linkletters were wondering where to go. Naturally, Van was right; I was still daffy enough to take on another of those periodic hangovers commonly called a "World Fair." A month later we arrived at the Golden Gate and the new job—still with no questions asked or answered about salary, responsibilities, or future. After all, we were rich and had no worries . . . we had almost two hundred dollars saved up.

Nineteen thirty-seven and nineteen thirty-eight went skidding by to the accompaniment of torchlight parades, bathing-beauty contests, stuffy civic banquets, and interminable speeches by civic leaders. And in case you've ever been bored stiff by a stuffed shirt, you ought to try writing for them and find out what the word "bored" really means. I wonder if anybody in public life ever writes his own speeches. I've worked on the pronouncements of vice-presidents of the United States, governors, senators, mayors, and a host of other responsible people, whose accomplishments certainly qualified them to speak for themselves but who usually mouth the words ground out like sausages by a flock of press agents and radio characters.

I remember one top official at one of the fairs whose

speeches invariably had to be cut at the last minute. How much they were cut and how quickly the job had to be done depended upon the color of his nose. As he walked through the door of the broadcasting booth my practiced eye would dart to that shining schnozz, and after a calculating peek at the shade I could tell whether he'd had anywhere from two to fifteen drinks under his belt. His normal reading rate was 185 words a minute, but for each drink over two the rate dropped fifteen words a minute. Sailing along under a real snootful, he'd pontificate deliberately and majestically at about one hundred words a minute. Many a time the entire fifteen minutes were absorbed in five pages out of a fifteen-page script, and since he never remembered what he was reading anyway, I found that I could use the same material over and over again.

One of the narrowest escapes I've had of missing a broadcast occurred on Christmas morning, 1938. A carillon had been built into the Tower of the Sun on Treasure Island and we had been invited to participate in a worldwide program of Christmas carols and hymns over the Mutual network. The broadcast was set for 8 A.M. December 25, and the rehearsal had been set for 7 A.M.

I awakened in my apartment near the Golden Gate at approximately seven-thirty. The normal driving time through the city across the bridge and down the ramp to Treasure Island was thirty minutes. There were no telephone connections on the island, and I could imagine the frantic radio crew waiting for me and the only copies of the script—which I'd thoughtfully kept.

With a record broad jump, I was out of bed, into a pair of slippers and an old dressing gown, and flying down the stairs to the car. Moments later I came leaping back up the stairs to get the car keys. Then downstairs I ran again. Once again I came screaming up the stairs—this time for the scripts. With uncombed hair flying in the breeze and bleary eyes staring through the windshield, I proceeded to pulverize all traffic laws. I arrived at Treasure Island with five minutes to spare. The deep, solemn bells of the carillon rang out the melody of "Holy Night." The narrator wore pajamas.

Japan, not to be outdone in this tremendous pageant of peace and happiness, came into the fair with the largest of all the foreign exhibits. A complete two-story building of bamboo had been constructed in Nippon, carefully numbered by the piece, dismantled, and shipped to Treasure Island for reassembly. One minor mishap occurred on the way across the Pacific when the S.S. *Tatsutu Maru* ran into a typhoon, shipped considerable water, and washed the numbers off all the bamboos. This made for lots of fun as the scores of bandy-legged little men imported for the building job scratched their heads over the gigantic jigsaw puzzle that had been sent them.

In the meantime it was my job to arrange a special broadcast from the deck of the Japanese ship which had anchored next to the fairgrounds. There on the main hatch on the foredeck, flanked by silk-hatted federal and state officials and toothy Nipponese diplomats, we went on the air to celebrate the first arrival of a foreign exhibit.

I had secured a gong four feet in diameter with which to give the opening of the show a proper oriental touch. Following this a Buddhist priest was to say a prayer in his native tongue on behalf of the fair. He was a little sawed-off fellow, who spoke no word of English, but who had been told carefully through interpreters, over and over again, that his prayer was to occupy not more than thirty seconds. Hissing and whistling acknowledgment, he had promised to observe this time limit. Again I impressed upon him through our chain of interpreters that the program was very full and very important and under no circumstances would he be allowed more than one half minute.

I might have known he would gum up the works. With eyes tightly closed, elbows drawn close to his sides, and finger tips compressed, he began a weird singsong chant. More than two hundred dignitaries listened solemnly, wedged firmly into the circle around the microphone, as the prayer ran on and on. The half-minute mark was reached and passed. A minute rolled by, then a minute and a half. Still no sign of any letup in the torrent of oriental jargon. I couldn't signal him because his eyes were shut. I couldn't switch to another mike because there wasn't one. With a decision born of desperation, I walked up closely behind him and stood waiting for the next whistling intake of air which punctuated his prayer. As the sibilant hiss began, I placed my hands under the little fellow's elbows and, hoisting him into the air, still praying steadily, I walked off. A startled gasp ran around the circle, and for a frightened moment I wondered whether the announcement of the severance of diplomatic relations would come first from Washington or Tokyo. But by then I was back at the mike, calmly announcing the first speaker on the program. The tension broke and the show went on as scheduled. I still wonder, sometimes, when I wake up during the quiet hours of the night, what Buddha thought of all this.

As the opening date of the fair approached, the work became more hectic and the responsibilities doubled and trebled. At the tender age of twenty-four my job was to organize a department which was in charge of scores of programs involving hundreds of thousands of dollars. Technical equipment had to be bought and set up, studios blueprinted and built, a staff of forty or fifty persons assembled, and a schedule of productions laid out for the networks and stations. On top of this I had been invited to write the theme spectacle of the fair, the *Cavalcade of the Golden West,* an outdoor spectacle to be staged at a cost of $350,000 and dedicated to presenting a history of the West in dramatic form.

In the midst of all this work and worry the fair proceeded to complicate my own and everyone else's job by appointing among its top officials a wild-haired, self-styled genius who promptly proceeded to foul up every constructive plan evolved. Through political connections and a set of bizarre circumstances too fantastic to relate, this refugee from a booby hatch was the man to whom I reported. I will not soon forget that fatal day when a peremptory call summoned me to his office for a conference. He began as he always did —in a manner calculated to win your immediate friendship and co-operation: "You are the lousiest radio director God ever made. You have no imagination, very little ability, and certainly no sense of the dramatic, or else we would have some really big productions planned for the fair."

I have never been noted for my ability to absorb this kind of punishment, and so it was only natural that I flared back at him and said, "What makes you think that you have any right to criticize me in any way about anything that has to do with show business? Instead of sitting there hurling abuse at the people who are trying to do a job around here, why don't you come up with one decent idea of your own?"

"Okay," he snapped, "you asked for it and here it is. If you had any brains of your own you'd have thought of it a long time ago. The San Francisco Bay Bridge is the biggest bridge in the world. It's dramatic, it's breathtaking, and, more than that, it could be the center of the most sensational broadcast ever heard on the radio. If you knew anything about engineering you would realize that every one of those cables is under tension like the strings of a giant harp, and by employing dozens of microphones hung up among the cables of the bridge at proper intervals, the wind from the Pacific could be heard playing a melody like a giant Aeolian harp. With a little experimentation you could pick out any melody you wanted and then the world would really have something to talk about."

I looked at him for a moment in utter disbelief. I thought he was kidding! I waited for the crinkle of a smile to break out around his lips as the immensity of this brainstorm sank home. But no, his belligerent look and triumphant attitude convinced me that he really believed in what he had just said.

"Well, if you aren't the silliest jerk I have ever listened to in my life, you'll do until one comes along." I turned and walked to the door. As I went out I called back over my shoulder, "You can consider the job of radio director as open. I quit!"

I was out of a job but full of plans and filled with a fierce desire to vindicate myself in the eyes of my friends among the staff at the fair. Within a week I'd sold my first commerical series to the Roma Wine Company. It was to be called "World's Fair Party" and was to originate every Saturday night from the Foods and Beverages Building at the fair and ride a network of thirty-five stations of the Mutual web. With this as my "bread-and-butter" account, I really went to work. One month later, when the fair opened its doors to the world on February 18, 1939, my script for the *Cavalcade* had been accepted over the bitter opposition of my "bridge-playing" friend. I had sold the fair itself a series of three programs a week, each one of which netted me as much as my previous salary as radio director.

I went on to sign up many of the big exhibits for special programs, and before long I found myself with from fifteen to twenty programs a week on the air, plus many other personal appearances on stage shows within the fairgrounds. Of course I had a *few* minor difficulties here and there. For one thing, I lost my battle to have a gigantic earthquake as the concluding scene of the *Cavalcade*. I wanted to reproduce the 1906 earthquake on the stage and at the same time operate a device under the five thousand-seat grandstand that would shake and quiver the entire structure. You can imagine what the San Francisco City Fathers thought of *that* one!

And then there was the time I staged a big broadcast for General Motors. It was to be an hour broadcast, and one of GM's top-drawer executives, Charles F. Kettering, was to fly from Detroit for the event.

The official in charge of General Motors Day at the fair instructed me to arrange the entire broadcast but to be sure and set aside forty minutes for an address by Mr. Kettering. I followed instructions.

Came the day of the broadcast. Fifteen minutes before air time I finally met Mr. Kettering. He was surrounded by a swarm of deferential sub-officials. A very gracious Mrs. Kettering accompanied him.

A passing introduction was all I rated, but it was not sufficient. "Just a moment, Mr. Kettering," I persisted. "If you don't mind, I'd like to double-check your part in the program."

The sub-officials glowered at my tone, but Mr. Kettering was friendly and co-operative. "Of course. How long am I to talk?"

"Forty minutes," I replied casually.

"Forty minutes! Who wants to hear me for forty minutes? I'll talk five." And he turned on his heel and walked off.

He might have been a very important man to the world, but to me at that moment he was just a guy who had wrecked my program. And I had to do something, quickly.

"But, Mr. Kettering," I sputtered, "my instructions were to give you forty minutes. The program's set. We can't change it. You've *got* to talk for forty minutes!"

"Do I?" he smiled. "What happens if I simply sit down at the end of five?" And again he turned away.

With seven minutes left before we started our hour-long program, I frantically turned my attentions to Mrs. Kettering.

"Golly, can't you help me?" I pleaded.

She smiled cheerfully and volunteered: "Have the orchestra play some music."

I explained no orchestra can play music unless that music is first cleared through the network's music department in New York, that orchestras have to rehearse before they can play, that a lot of other complicated matters must be considered before the orchestra plays music.

"No," I sighed, "the orchestra can't play that much music. Your husband has just got to talk for forty minutes, that's all."

"In that case," she said, "I don't know what to tell you to do."

I was desperate and showed it. There was one last straw and I grasped it.

"Mrs. Kettering," I muttered, "our orchestra can play 'Home, Sweet Home.' Do you like 'Home, Sweet Home'?"

"Why, yes," she said promptly. "It's one of my favorites."

"Mrs. Kettering, I promise you that unless you can persuade your husband to talk for at least thirty-five minutes, you'll hear 'Home, Sweet Home' played continuously and consecutively fourteen times." With that I hurried to the microphone and made my introductory remarks. The band began to play. A few minutes later I introduced Mr. Charles F. Kettering. His wife had spoken firmly to him.

Mr. Kettering was a very intelligent man. He talked for thirty-five minutes.

One Foot in Heaven

EVER SINCE I COULD REMEMBER, I HAD BEEN AFRAID OF Hollywood.

I had the same feeling of apprehension that a small boy has for a haunted house. He wants to go, but . . .

From the moment I first decided on radio as a career, I had known that someday I must try to crash Hollywood. It is the symbol of success; it represents the ultimate in opportunity.

It is also the graveyard of the Unknown Performer.

Compared to Hollywood, the India caste system is a society of free souls living in simple democratic bliss. Heaven help the person with no job or visible source of income. He is an untouchable.

Everyone at KGB in San Diego dreamed of the time when he would get the nod from KHJ, the Mutual network headquarters in Hollywood. In many respects it was like the order to go over the top in the front lines; it was what we were training for, striving for, and intended for, and it might very well be The End.

That is why I waited eight long years before making my bid. I had been a chief announcer, a program director, a radio director, and a regional network star. I had been successful in San Diego, Dallas, and San Francisco. I had a network commercial that had been on the air for one sponsor steadily for two years. And I moved south from the Golden Gate with no favors or jobs to ask of anyone.

And yet I was scared stiff.

All those years of hearing vicious whispers of cutthroat politics, stories of professional intrigues that spread out along the network like devil grass in a garden, had left their mark on my imagination. In fact, I had so little confidence in the stability of my future there that I left a small anchor to windward: five hundred miles to windward, to be exact, for I never relinquished my local Sunday-night-interview program in San Francisco. I took a lot of kidding from my Hollywood colleagues, but each week I flew north to sell the "House of Lucky Wedding Rings," even though the fee for a single-station broadcast did little more than cover expenses. It meant that my business friends in that wonderful city by the Golden Gate were contacted regularly, and my listening audience in the Bay area was scarcely aware that I had moved away.

Fulfilling my worst expectations, the first thing that happened in Hollywood was the loss of my network commercial. The "What Do You Think?" show exploded when the crackpot radical eulogized Hitler and disintegrated the Linkletter-Roma Wine contract. I tried for several months to reassemble the pieces, but I could do no better than "all the King's horses."

Then followed months of agonizing "sustaining" programs. These are shows built by the networks and put on the air in the dim hope that somebody, somewhere, will hear them and sign up as the sponsor. The fees are ridiculously low; in many cases less than one tenth the price of a commercially sponsored performance. The broadcast time consists of leftover scraps which remain after the sponsors pick out the best listening hours for their programs. The artist often feels that he's just marking time until the network can think of something better to do.

All at once a miracle happened. My sustaining program, called "Who, What, Where, and Why," was sold to the Los Angeles *Times*. I was on the air over KNX each week with a local sponsor, to be true, but one of the most powerful in the West. At last, my friends told me, I was really established and ready to go places. But still that weekly trip to San Francisco was never canceled. . . .

And oh, how glad I was that I had not gone overboard because of my new sponsor. A few weeks later a nationally known commercial came through from New York, taking my time, and leaving us just one open half hour to move to—opposite Bob Hope.

The *Times* took one look at the opposition and again I was a "sustaining" star!

My next big venture was a comedy series called "Look Who's Here!" I was the star. We had a band, guest, comedy writers, and lots of jokes. In fact, we had everything but a good show, and a sponsor.

It was during this painful indoctrination into scripted comedy shows that I acquired a deep sympathy for comics and their writers. I can conceive of nothing so nerve-jangling as a script filled with jokes which may or may not produce laughs. One word out of place in the routine, one tiny fraction of a second off in the timing of the boff line, one distracting movement by anyone on stage during the pay-off . . . and the gag lies there dead. So does the funnyman.

I also learned that the funniest gag lines in a rehearsal room often are the unfunniest when you're in front of a strange audience. And the most innocent remarks will send the customers into a laughing jag.

In brief, I learned that I should stick to my own specialty, that an ad-lib comedy show with people is NOT a qualifying test for a written, timed comedy show with a script.

That's why we dreamed up a show called "Shell Goes to a Party." This one was to be the *pièce de résistance*—the big one that skyrockets Linkletter to the top—and sure enough, it did perform exactly like a skyrocket . . . right to the final crash to earth.

The idea was sound, and I still believe it could be worked.

We proposed to attend all kinds of parties and to describe them in a thirty-minute broadcast. Thus our listeners would accompany us to a different kind of a party in a different location each week: beach clambakes, dude-ranch roundups, modest birthday celebrations, wedding anniversaries, and so on. Anyone giving a party anywhere could write us and we would pick the interesting ones for a remote-control show. Our CBS network lines would be run out to the location; I would arrange party games and prizes to suit the occasion and a guest list; then we would supply a half hour of entertainment to both the party guests and the listeners, courtesy of the sponsor.

Before I go any further, I think you should know something about the way in which radio shows are actually assembled, auditioned, sold, and put on the air.

In the early days of radio the stations and networks themselves came up with the original ideas for programs and attempted to sell them to sponsors complete with star, music, writers, and guests. After a suitable program had been put together, a network salesman would begin calling on advertising agencies in hope of interesting them in presenting it to a firm that was going to advertise on the radio. The agency executives did the actual selling of the program to their own clients and were responsible for recommending the right day and hour for the presentation of the show. For this they received fifteen per cent of the cost of the radio time and fifteen per cent of the cost of the talent.

Nowadays most big-time programs are put together by the agencies or by individuals who call themselves independent producers. Most programs are called "packages" because every ingredient of the show is wrapped up by the agency or producer and presented with a single price tag. For instance, if the Joe Doakes Variety show is sold, the price may be a flat $10,000 per week. Within this price the producer must arrange his various costs in order to make his own profit.

In the case of my "Shell Goes to a Party" idea, the Columbia network did all the underwriting of costs and owned the program lock, stock, and Linkletter. One of the largest agencies in the country, the J. Walter Thompson Company, was the middleman in the deal, and the sponsor, naturally, was to be the Shell Oil Company.

At this point, in the sale of a show, it is customary to give what is known as an "audition," although it is actually a holdover from the days of the Inquisition so far as the artist is concerned. Auditions are nerve-racking and unfair even to the most veteran of performers, whether "live" or "transcribed."

The "live" variety is by far the worst. In this type the agency and prospective sponsor are invited to actually attend the program, watch it from a special booth, and then criticize it. The knowledge that anywhere from five to fifty self-appointed judges are listening to every word, every inflection, and each syllable is enough to guarantee that you will NOT do your best!

The "transcribed" audition is much easier on the performer. With this method, the show is recorded on a transcription. If there are any mistakes while it is being done, the program can be stopped, a new record put on, and the whole thing done over again. Even after it has all been transcribed, the engineers can go back over it and cut out words, phrases, or even entire sections which may not be satisfactory. Then, when the entire program is in perfect shape "on wax," it is taken to the office of the agency or sponsor and played there over a loud-speaker at the convenience of the executives.

Bing Crosby was the first important artist to insist that all of his actual broadcasts be transcribed. He thus began a trend that has changed radio from a "live" to a predominantly "canned" medium. And he did it for two important reasons: first, as I have pointed out, the assurance of a perfect program. When recorded, you can go back and cut out dull portions, featuring the bright spots. As I remember it, in one

of Bing's first programs in his Philco series Bob Hope was
the guest star and the actual program ran for forty-seven
minutes. A lot of this was ad-lib fun and banter, and the
performers didn't have a worry in the world. If they ran over,
the length could be cut out of the record mechanically. If
they said something wrong or inane, that remark, or the entire
routine around it, could be eliminated. Thus the show had
an easy, relaxed pace which makes for good fun at the
receiver. In the second place, by transcribing his shows, Bing
could do three or four or even more programs in the space of
a week. Then he would be free to concentrate on his pictures,
his golf, or his travels. Also, in case of sickness or accident,
there would always be time to make substitutions because
of the supply of recorded programs held in reserve.

At any rate, to get back to my own problems with the
"Shell Party," we had decided to make an audition record
of a fraternity barn dance at U.S.C. There, before a howling
mob of costumed collegians, I M.C.'d a program that lasted
a full hour. It was a genuine "clambake," which, translated
freely, means a jumble of confusion, both good and bad.
However, we had no worries, because we knew that the
buyers would never hear it the way it first went on that
transcription.

I can remember the qualms I had about some of the mishaps that occurred at this fraternity party, and wondering
what I would have done if we had been on the air and un-
able to play around with a recording AFTER the show was
over.

But we fashioned a hilarious half-hour audition record and
the program was sold successfully to Shell.

The first thirteen weeks were to be Pacific Coast releases
with a full transcontinental network contingent on the way
the show was going. I was sitting on top of the world. This
was the first time in seven years that anyone had sold the
powerful oil company, and my name was being plastered
around in nice, big, fat black letters. I was touring the coast

speaking to dealer meetings. The network was patting itself
on the back. But I still kept my San Francisco show. . . .

Then came the first party broadcast.

It was to originate at the swank Somerset House on the
occasion of the annual party of the Southern California
Aviation Country Club, and a host of celebrities were to be
on hand for the fun.

The show was scheduled to hit the air at 8:30 P.M., but I
was there at six-thirty—just to be sure of everything.

The engineers had the lines hooked up. The producers
had checked all prizes. The script had been marked and
corrected. The advertising executives from the agency and
the sponsors were beginning to arrive on the scene.

And then the bar opened.

By seven-thirty the guests who had arrived for cocktails
before dinner were getting plenty of altitude. They were
wealthy executives who owned their own planes and flew
them as a hobby. They were neither awed by the sight of
a microphone nor impressed by the fact that their annual
party was to be on the air. Their one concern was to get
close enough to the bar to fuel up for what apparently was
to be a round-the-world, non-stop trip.

Sweat broke all over my body as I realized what was happening to my first important show even BEFORE it went
on the air.

Alerting my producer to the danger, we both made a
search for the club president, who had promised us every
co-operation. We HAD to have the bar closed, or at least
curtailed, until after the program!

"Oh, don't worry, boys!" He smiled reassuringly at us.
"The men of this club know how to hold their liquor, and
besides, it's eight o'clock already. Just another half hour.
What can happen?"

Yeah! What could happen!

Three minutes before air time the place was a bedlam.
Old pals were "old-palling" at the tops of their voices. The

president by this time was no more able to get the co-operation of the membership than we had been able to get his
serious attention a half hour before.

"Jim! Jim, old pal! Don't worry about a lil broadcast!
It'll be all right. You c'n count on ush every time, Jim! Come
on over and have a lil drink!"

In complete desperation, I pulled a table out to the middle
of the floor and jumped on it. Waving a script in one hand
and an open napkin in the other, I shouted at the top of my
lungs for silence.

The sight of this big fellow apparently gone berserk

silenced the crowd for the moment I needed to announce that in just thirty seconds we would be broadcasting over CBS and the honor of their club was at stake. Would everybody please take a seat because two of their own members were about to take part in the show and those two were none other than Amos 'n' Andy!

It worked. The crowd grabbed chairs, grouped themselves around tables, and we were on the air with no more than five seconds to spare.

Dear old Charley Correll and Freeman Gosden came through like million-carat sparklers. They were sober and sympathetic during the impromptu show, and they held the crowd while our stunt developed into the final boff. And then, as I struggled with other stunts and less show-wise participants, the conversational noise slowly began to build, build, and build. Finally the place was a shambles again, with no more attention being paid me or my show than to a bus boy. I realized that we could never again regain the ear of the gang, so I tried to "save face" with our listeners by loudly instructing the guests to "go right ahead with the party just as if we weren't here with the microphone, because we want the radio audience to catch a real picture of the fun and frivolity."

Centuries later we reached nine o'clock and the sign-off. I sat down to mop my dripping face and await the verdict of the agency, client, and network masterminds who had gone out to their car radios to catch the show from a listener's angle.

Sure enough, they came bustling in with the congratulations that are offered a performer after the first show—no matter how much of a stinker it is—and after a few highballs and the eloquent praise of the execs, I actually began to believe that maybe I had pulled one out of the fire. Somehow, the enthusiasm of a show infects everyone close to it until the true perspective is lost in a fog of ecstasy.

The next day things were different.

From the boys and girls who had stayed home to listen came the objective, caustic comments that cut you down to size. Teletypes from the San Francisco home office confirmed my own private suspicions. But we had learned our lesson, we felt, and no more chances would be taken on the next show.

The second week was to be a beach party on the shores of the Pacific near Santa Monica. We enlisted the aid of the life guards and built a huge bonfire; we had mountains of wienies and marshmallows, and a guest list of about fifty people who could be counted on to "give" with the applause and laughs. We had as a special guest "Miss America of 1941," and as a special surprise we were going to throw her into the ocean and thus break the old tradition of a bathing beauty never wetting her suit.

Every minute detail, every possible emergency, had been considered. This time nothing could go wrong.

Two hours before broadcast time a strong west wind blew up and tiny sand particles began flying through the air. It was an ill wind and it blew absolutely no good.

One hour before broadcast time the invited guest list had miraculously swelled from fifty to four times that many, including a gang of young beach kids who were studying to be juvenile delinquents.

Thirty minutes before broadcast time the public-address amplifier blew out, leaving me to shout necessary directions. I was faced with a broadcast in which none of the conversation would be heard by the crowd around the microphone. What sound would not be swallowed up in the open air would be blown away by the breeze!

But in spite of these unexpected disasters we bubbled our way through a fair-to-middling show until the final spot. It was here that I was to interview Miss America until, at a certain signal, my assistants would pick up that young glamour girl and carry her twenty-five yards down to the waves. I would be following with my portable microphone attached to a long cable that would permit me to run after them and catch the actual splash as she hit the water.

All went well until the mad chase for the waves began. In the pitch-darkness outside the ring of bonfire light I failed to see an old log which was waiting there to snare my mike cable.

My gay stream of breathless conversation came to an abrupt and tragic halt midway to the water. The microphone whipped to a dead stop and I flew through the air, arms and legs flailing like a demented helicopter.

Then came a mad scramble to find the "network" lost there in the seaweed-studded darkness. I couldn't say anything I really thought for fear the mike would be near enough to pick it up. The radio audience all this time must have concluded I had dived headlong into the Pacific after Miss America.

When we had finally located the mike and ended the show, I was convinced that I had at long last discovered the program that would send me to an old man's grave before another week had passed.

It almost did.

The next morning there was a brief wire from the president of Shell. It stated succinctly:

CANCEL THE PROGRAM. PAY OFF LINKLETTER. TERMINATE THE NETWORK TIME.

If that isn't a quick ticket, one way only, to the radio cemetery, it'll do till a better comes along.

Here was a show touted to go transcontinentally over a major network, sponsored by one of the biggest corporations in the world, and produced by the largest advertising agency in the business: washed out after two weeks! With that kind of a record back of me, I could probably hope to get a job someday, after ten or fifteen years of probation, reading a time signal over a ten-watt station in Penwiper, Nebraska, after midnight.

And yet, as I look back over those miserable weeks, I can't see how I could have done any differently no matter how earnestly I tried. The "breaks" were running in the wrong direction, and all the good intentions in the world were of no avail. The jinx of Hollywood was working twenty-four hours a day. Everything I tried seemed destined to failure.

Then I met John Guedel. John is now my partner, in both "People Are Funny" and "House Party." He also is the producer of both shows. In addition to which he is very interesting, bald, and a pixy. Let me tell you more about him.

John once felt the urge to write. He had received eighty-five magazine rejection slips before his first sale to *True Confessions* for fifteen dollars. Followed a "long string" of sales (two more, he admits). Then he worked for a steel-house company, a landscape gardener, and finally achieved moderate success after the New Year's Day flood of 1934; he became a construction engineer for the city of Beverly Hills. His duties: to clean debris from the sewers!

During this period John renewed acquaintanceship with an old high-school friend who liked to draw cartoons. They joined forces, Guedel writing the funny jokes beneath the drawings. They submitted their cartoons to several syndicates and finally received a positive answer from the huge Newspaper Enterprise Association. An editor of that syndicate wanted the man who wrote the jokes to go to Cleveland and write a humorous column on the news of the day! Guedel's column shortly was syndicated to 723 papers!

In one of his columns he wrote about a news item that stated a fish with bulging eyes had appeared off the California coast and nobody could understand why. Guedel suggested the fish probably figured if Irvin S. Cobb could act in the movies, so could he, the fish! Mr. Cobb was acting for Hal

Roach at the time, and the latter became intrigued by the piece in the column. He wrote John, asked if he'd like to try writing for the movies.

That's Hollywood for you: Guedel had to go to Cleveland to land a job in his own back yard! At any rate, he stayed with Roach for a year and a half writing Our Gang and Laurel and Hardy comedies.

In 1943 John had an original idea for a screenplay. He outlined his idea, called it *Tornado*, and had his agent submit it to all of the major film companies. None were interested. So Guedel, by this time wise to the ways of Hollywood, had the outline published in the form of a book. Only twenty-five copies were printed. Only one was enough. The agent took the published volume around to the studios again, and this time Paramount snapped it up. (It was exactly the same story all had previously refused!) And the story was produced with Chester Morris and Nancy Kelly in the leading roles. On the screen flashed the credit: "From the novel by John Guedel!"

From movies he passed into the advertising business and became interested in radio when his "Pull Over, Neighbor" program became a success. Today John Guedel Productions employs fifty-nine people, has offices in our own building in Hollywood, handles seventeen coast-to-coast weekly half-hour programs.

This, then, is my partner. You can see that he is the possessor of a mighty imagination.

Seldom in show business is there such a perfect working partnership as that which exists between John and myself. Each complements the other perfectly, and in nineteen years I can't recall a serious disagreement on any of the hundreds of details that perpetually arise to plague producers.

I first met him at the Hollywood Brown Derby. Our meeting had been previously arranged by a mutual friend, Bruce Eells, then a salesman for the Mutual Broadcasting System. Bruce decided that I had something to offer John and that John had talents that would work in harmony with mine. Neither of us had ever seen the other. After that lunch date we have never been separated. It was in 1940.

John had an idea for a psychology show, based more or less on his "Pull Over, Neighbor" idea. The master of ceremonies would work with a psychologist who could scientifically and on the spot analyze people and their reactions to various questions and stunts. I had brought with me from San Francisco an idea for a psychology show which I called "Meet Yourself." The two ideas were more or less the same in that a pseudo-scientific approach was used within the bounds of good showmanship.

As we sat in the Derby talking over our ideas, John doodled with a pencil on the tablecloth. He looked at the other luncheon guests in the famous establishment, noted how some were also doodling on napkins, how others were half listening to their table companions, and in general studied the actions of a crowd of several hundred people. Then he mused, half to himself, "Y'know . . . people are funny!"

That was it . . . the idea we were looking for, with a natural title. We pooled our thoughts on an audience-participation program, called it "People Are Funny," and each contributed fifteen dollars of our meager funds for an audition record. From that original investment of thirty dollars John and I have developed a business that brings in more than a quarter of a million a year! Yes . . . people are funny. And profitable, too!

An old friend, Professor Milton Metfessel, of the University of Southern California, was called in as a psychology counselor and the three of us worked out the format for our new show. We produced a trial, nonbroadcast audition recording at the NBC studios in the early part of 1941.

We discovered that the purely educational and scholarly approach to people through scientific tests was not much fun, while the zany, pseudo-scientific gadgets and games were on a par with anything we'd ever heard along audience-participation lines.

So we cut out the professor's parts, the analysis charts, and inserted in their place some original stunts out of the previous Guedel opus, "Pull Over, Neighbor." This was the first game show that I ever heard about in radio and, to the best of my knowledge, is the grandpappy of all the present audience-participation stunt shows. It started in early 1938 and continued until a few months before our partnership began. It had featured an M.C. named Art Baker, and he was included in our recorded audition package. Thus the "People Are Funny" production was a show with two stars, which I should have known could lead only to trouble.

Sure enough, at the end of the first five weeks, Baker suddenly announced that he was incompatible with me and would either handle the show alone or would quit. Guedel and I, after a hasty consultation, notified the agency, in Chicago, that Baker was quitting and that I would do the show alone.

But here old Witch Fate was spinning her web counter-Linkletter again, because word came back from Chicago headquarters that Baker was the fair-haired boy and that to fire him would jeopardize the entire show at that early period in its growth. After all, we were only a summer "fill-in" and a long way from being a solid member of the NBC family.

Guedel had resigned from a Los Angeles agency job and gambled everything on this new partnership of ours, and I felt that rather than lose our first transcontinental venture I should withdraw from the program, in spite of the obvious unfairness of Baker's demands.

Filled with bitterness and the acid of defeat, I left my first big-time show behind and told Guedel to hold the fort alone.

I was through with Hollywood.

This last blow was too much to take on top of everything

else that had come my way during the year and a half in southern California.

I packed up my family and moved back to San Francisco. Back to the wonderful, friendly city by the Golden Gate where I had kept my following through that solitary local show to which I had flown north each week.

Professionally I was a question mark. I had gone forth to the Big Battle with flags flying and sponsors applauding . . . and now I was sneaking back with bruises and very little else. Perhaps I was meant for the local station programs. Perhaps my talents were too few.

I went over every experience, every program effort that I had put forth in Hollywood. I analyzed, diagramed, and studied each step and each failure. And then I decided that it had been an experience that I could profit by if I didn't lose confidence or courage.

Girding my mental loins, I decided to build another inventory of program firepower, and the NEXT time I laid siege to Hollywood it would be a different story.

The next two years were tough. I set out to do anything and everything in radio that would give me experience and money. Nothing was too much work or trouble. No station was too small if the program was right. The measuring rod by which I gauged each new offer was this: What can it do to help me become a better broadcaster?

I did interview shows on street corners, open forum shows in theaters, gag shows from hotel lobbies, "platter" shows with running patter, spelling bees, news commentaries, and variety programs. Some weeks I would do as many as twenty-one commercial broadcasts, all of which I conceived, wrote, produced, and M.C.'d. Some of them were over tiny independent stations, others over fifty-thousand-watt powerhouses, and still others over complete West Coast networks.

Slugging away alongside of me on the comeback trail was a pugnacious little Irishman named Larry Allen who had called me up during my blacker moments to say that he was betting I'd make it the hard way. Could he come along for the ride? Ride? Well, not exactly. It was more like a treadmill with a non-stop schedule attached. As my new manager, Larry was entitled to ten per cent of everything I made, but some of the jobs were so skimpy that he'd refuse to take a nickel and told me there'd be plenty of time for him when we were in the chips. This sublime confidence in the future pulled me through more than one bad time and sent me out to frolic and kid before the Annual Meeting of the Daughters of the Founders of Milpetas, while wondering deep down if Hollywood and its transcontinental hookups really existed in the same world with such small-time efforts.

Then one day Larry came bursting over the phone with news that the American Broadcasting Company was set to give me a Pacific Coast network five afternoons a week if we could come up with a good show.

"How much time do we have?" I asked breathlessly. "A week or two?"

"A week!" Allen shouted. "We have an appointment in thirty minutes! Dream up some gimmicks and ad-lib your way through this first meeting. Any time you get stuck I'll kick over a wastebasket. We'll murder 'em."

And I guess we did, because two weeks later I was a network broadcaster again and on my way back to Heartbreak Hollow.

In the meantime I was contributing gags, situations, and ideas to "People Are Funny" through weekly letters to Guedel. Our partnership survived the bitter decisions, and we unflaggingly worked to build the show into a strong keystone of the sponsor's advertising structure.

Then, after more than a year of waiting, the show changed into the "New People Are Funny" program, Mr. Baker was through, and I was back on the air with my own nighttime commercial, coast to coast over NBC.

I had one foot in Heaven.

Stars Don't Always Twinkle

THE FIVE KOZAL BROTHERS WERE WAR VETERANS. THEY'D represented a patriotic family in the Army, Navy, and Marines. One had even been a paratrooper, with a record that included a drop on Corregidor to rescue that bastion from the Japs.

When all the Kozals had been discharged from the service, they planned fulfillment of a collective dream: to go into business for themselves. Pooling their service savings, they purchased equipment for a hot-dog stand!

Now, opening a hot-dog stand in Hollywood is somewhat the same as planting a tree in Sequoia National Park. The competition is terrific. Clearly it was a case for Old Doc Linkletter and his "People Are Funny" clinic. We held a spirited consultation, my staff and I. All agreed something should be done to assist these ex-servicemen in their postwar venture.

Came the night of Friday, January 31. From the studio audience an attractive young wife of an Army Air Corps captain was chosen. While he gazed adoringly from his seat in the crowd, I asked her if she'd ever heard of a big Hollywood première, with lights and stars and photographers and radio announcers and crowds and excitement. She said she had. "Well," I continued, "tonight you're going to attend a real world première with all the trimmings.

"What's more, you'll not only *attend* the première, but you'll actually be in charge of it! We want *you* to go down there now and be our representative. They're installing a microphone right this minute. When you get there, you take over. We'll get the signal when you're ready, and 'People Are Funny' will switch to you. Talk to the people in the crowd, describe the searchlights . . . give us every detail. Pay particular attention to what the women are wearing. You're going to be the famous Hollywood commentator, Louella Hopper."

Our attractive young contestant was bubbling over. Almost breathlessly she asked, "Where is the première happening?"

"You know where Grauman's Chinese Theatre is?"

"Yes."

"Well, about six blocks down the street from there a brand-new hot-dog stand is having its world première. And that's where you're going!"

While the crowd roared at her dismay, I waved good-by and away she went on her new job.

A few minutes later she arrived at the location of the première. Sure enough, hundreds of curious people were packed along the sidewalk of Sunset Boulevard. Sure enough, searchlights examined the sky. Sure enough, half a dozen photographers banged their flash bulbs when she stepped from her car. And sure enough . . . it *was* a hot-dog stand!

A platoon of Los Angeles police officers attended the crowd as our contestant took up her duties at the microphone. She was one of the best amateur announcers I have ever heard. She described the ten-stool hot-dog stand. She chatted with a lady from the crowd. She gave a surprisingly good picture of the lights and the passing traffic. Then she gasped in amazement at a shiny black limousine that purred to a stop at the curb. From it stepped . . . Roy Rogers! Doffing his ten-gallon hat, smiling the world-famous Rogers smile, the affable Roy ambled up to the microphone. Our contestant, flabbergasted, did the best she could. Roy gabbed merrily for a minute or two and then walked into the stand and ordered a hot dog.

Another big limousine purred to the curb. Out stepped a gracious, smiling Judy Canova. The crowd let up a whoop of delight. Things were sure as hell happening around *here* tonight!

Judy spoke her piece and joined Roy at the lunch counter. Our fair contestant's jaw dropped in disbelief.

Up purred another limousine. Out stepped Bob Burns, the amiable Arkansas philosopher. He bowed to the crowd, posed a second for the photographers, and joined our by now "authority" at the microphone. It is a good thing Bob Burns was one of the best ad-libbers in radio, for he found it necessary to do all the talking; our contestant was virtually speechless.

Still another black limousine gently slid to the curb. And to the thunder of approval from the crowd, out stepped Red Skelton. He was having a picnic over the whole thing. Red took over from there.

By this time our contestant had found the remains of her voice. With Red assisting, she conducted an interview that will go down in radio annals as unique, to say the least. At its conclusion Skelton assumed a sitting posture on a fourth stool in the hot-dog stand.

Another black limousine purred up to the curb. The waiting policeman opened the door. Out stepped a gorgeous Earl Carroll beauty in stunning evening clothes. And on her arm, with a smile as wide as the Grand Canyon, was an Army Air Corps captain—our contestant's husband!

Needless to say, the Kozal Hot Dog Stand was in business. And five deserving veterans were on their way in the lunch-counter world.

This was quite an elaborate stunt, even for "People Are Funny." We had to make sure of a crowd, photographers, remote broadcasting lines, five big limousines, and dozens of other details. And it was up to us to induce five top stars to participate. Without them the stunt would have laid an egg big enough to provide sandwiches for the Kozal brothers for the rest of their lives.

We couldn't afford to pay our guest stars. Their fees would have amounted to more than twenty-five thousand dollars. Yet these servicemen represented the millions of young Americans struggling to start a new life, so—we asked the guest stars to help out . . . for nothing! Roy Rogers, Judy Canova, Bob Burns, and Red Skelton were the first ones we asked. And every one agreed with a smile and without a murmur of protest. When the cause is just, Hollywood has a heart as big as the Pacific Ocean.

It may seem strange, but famous Hollywood stars usually don't fit in too well with our type of show. And for a variety of reasons we don't plan many stunts that employ a big-name star.

Celebrities are by far the most difficult people to interview without scripts. Professional entertainers are many times harder to talk to on the air than people who have never stood up to introduce a guest at the local Club for the Advancement of Pack Rats!

The reason is simple. The "big name" is on the spot. He has a reputation to protect or enhance, and his appearance may lose him friends and even future engagements. More often than not he has made his mark on the stage, screen, or radio by the use of carefully prepared scripts which have been arduously rehearsed and polished under skilled direction.

In his own specialized medium the star has the same easy familiarity that an ad-libber enjoys in an unrehearsed show; and on his own program the "pro" has the relaxed delivery that comes with the assurance that his writing staff knows his style and has carefully blocked out the continuity for his benefit. Without any of these "props," and facing a man whose reputation for extemporaneous repartee has been built up after years of catch-as-catch-can practice, you can't blame him for feeling apprehensive on "People Are Funny" . . . he doesn't know what is going to happen!

Two of the most nervous, jittery stars ever to face me across a microphone were Amos 'n' Andy. Perfectionists in their art, absolutely nerveless in their own studio with their own script, they were as jumpy as a bridegroom at a shotgun wedding when the "On the Air" sign lit up at the "People Are Funny" program.

We had a wonderful stunt rigged in which a contestant was to coach several other "volunteers" in the art of impersonating famous radio stars. He was a young accountant from Massachusetts, and after a quick "hello" I sent him off-stage to study a list of the people he was to impersonate.

While he was out of hearing I revealed to the listeners that the two "volunteers" he would be coaching were actually Freeman Gosden and Charles Correll—Amos 'n' Andy—masters of every voice change and mimics par excellence. By the time we had explained the hoax and called the unsuspecting guest back before the microphone, our two stars were about the color of a newborn guppy.

Without scripts and working at a mike with an accountant, they were understandably apprehensive. But, as you can guess, they carried off their parts flawlessly . . . and ran through a series of deliberately amateurish attempts to imitate Walter Winchell, Ned Sparks, Edward G. Robinson, and Lionel Barrymore. When the "coach" finally got around on our written list of suggestions to the characters of Kingfish, Lightnin', et cetera, he was going strong. He struggled with the two inept men before him until finally, at my signal, they burst into a perfect routine of Amos 'n' Andy characters while the young fellow stood there, a picture of awe-struck consternation. When he finally learned whom he'd been teaching to act on the radio, he almost fainted. And our two famous guests had actually begun to enjoy their unrehearsed visit.

Certainly one of the last stars you would ever expect to get the jitters is that rough, tough boss of the underworld, the thick-skinned, hard-eyed skipper, the unruffled secret-service operator: Edward G. Robinson.

I've seen him standing nervously in the wings of the San Francisco Opera House sweating like a longshoreman.

Here was a really unusual case. Eddie told me that years ago he had been a traveling sales executive who had been paid to address all kinds of luncheons, banquets, sales meetings, and other gatherings. He could toss off an impromptu pep talk at the drop of a quota. Then he'd entered stage work, gone on to his tremendous success on the screen, and as the years passed he memorized every word that he spoke while performing before the camera. The old facility was lost, and when he was suddenly called to speak he found that he was afflicted with the same stage fright that plagues the rawest amateur.

He had been watching me kid around in the spotlight, and the questions he fired at me during the "breather" in the wings made me suspect that he was "giving me the business." But one close look at his taut face was enough assurance—"Little Caesar" really had the shakes!

A few moments later he was out on the stage giving a sincere, smooth performance utterly at variance with the picture of despair he had presented before walking out for his bit. That's the test of a real showman.

A performer like Eddie Cantor, on the other hand, is equally at home with script or without. His thousands of personal appearances over the years have given him such a rich backlog of material that no matter what the occasion he can pull out of his memory a story or a gag that fits the bill. Like other great comedians who have stayed on top for more than a decade, he is so full of his subject that he can spout comedy routines about any given subject in a way that sounds completely impromptu.

But although it is ad-libbed on the spur of the moment, it is really not extemporaneous. It is unconscious adaptation of basic comedy formulae to the situation, with additions of new names or locales to suit the audience. Eddie not only consented to appear with me on a coast-to-coast show (the

"House Party") with no rehearsal or preparation whatsoever, but he quickly agreed to go with me into the aisles and answer any questions tossed his way by the visitors. Every answer was a jewel: either twisted to lead into a sure-fire gag that he'd used before or turned into a routine that paid off with some equally "boff" joke element.

What many top performers have forgotten with their artificial comedy situations and carefully "hypoed" characterizations is that genuine humor is as simple and elemental as the back-fence chitchat of a couple of neighbors. Ozzie and Harriet have raised the commonplace to new highs in comedy entertainment. And this is most certainly the basis for all ad-lib interview programs.

Ask the average big-name artist if his wife helps him to select his clothes and he'll answer a simple "yes" or "no" with very little elaboration in either words or inflections. But ask this of your man-in-the-audience, and the chances are he'll pipe up with an indignant "Heck no, I pick 'em out and I pay for 'em" . . . or an embarrassed "Well, yes, in a way . . . that is . . . she suggests what SHE thinks would be right, and then I buy it."

But what if the person in the audience is a "dope" who has never been anywhere of interest, done anything worth hearing about, or has a personality like a pickled octopus? What can you do with a dud like that?

Well, you shouldn't have picked him in the first place, but if you ARE stuck with him, make the visit as short as possible. There is another way of pulling a hot one like this out of the ether: if the subject you're talking *to* is dull, pick a subject to talk *about* that has zing. In other words, dive into a topic that will make the *listener* sit up and take part in the show. If it's about a husband beating a wife, or a mother spoiling her child, or a man being a better cook than a woman, you can bet it won't make any difference to the average family listening in whether your interviewee has a brilliant answer or not; they'll be answering you or him or each other so intently, whether out loud or to themselves, that your show will leap over the spot of verbal dry rot.

It's amazing how seldom you encounter a *volunteer* who doesn't have something to say that will give you a laugh, or a peg to hang a laugh on. It's the ones who want to go *on* talking that cause the real trouble,

I'll never forget one sweet little lady, white-haired, bright-eyed, and a bottomless well of words, who almost ran away with my program. She heard my opening question, "Where are you from?" and took it from there.

"Dallas, Texas! The loveliest city you could pick to raise a family. Pa and me moved there from Pittsburgh just after we was married and we've raised eleven children there—"

"Oh, fine." I jumped into what I thought was a pause for breath.

"That's not all." She raised her voice triumphantly. "There's the grandchildren; four curly-headed little boys who just live to be spoiled . . . and don't think I don't spoil 'em every chance I get."

"Do you—"

"Grandmas have a right to do a little extra spoiling after all the trouble they've gone to a-raisin' their own, don't you think?"

"Well . . ."

"Of course I *knew* you'd agree, Mr. Linkletter. You look like such a good, kind father yourself. But don't forget, too much freedom these days is ruining a lot of young folks, so be sure to spend plenty of time at home with yours. . . ."

This went on and on, past the time allotted for our "oldest grandmother," past the time for the commercial, and the audience by this time was howling as they caught on to my dilemma.

Any rudeness would have spoiled the whole show, aroused the ire of our listeners, and undone all the good that the time so far had accomplished. Yet it was essential that I do *some-*

thing to get the program back on its schedule. This is one of the most ticklish spots in the business.

I motioned to the assistant who was holding a shiny electric iron behind him to move over next to me. I reached around, snatched the prize, and suddenly, when she paused for breath, held it before her while the audience "oh'd" and "ah'd" their delight, and then jumped in to say this gorgeous gadget was all hers for being our oldest grandmother of the day, and congratulations, and good-by.

While saying these farewell words I walked away with the microphone, and as the crowd applauded, she looked around a little helplessly and then sat down, still chock-full of unspoken words.

I've been talking about *difficulties* in interviewing. Now let's introduce the folks who are the *easiest,* most *enjoyable* guests: the children! In a subsequent chapter I will describe some of the wonderful times I've had with youngsters at the "House Party," and some of the sensational answers I've received. But let me emphasize now that kiddies from four to twelve are the perfect age and in the ideal condition for unrehearsed interviews.

To begin with, they are totally frank and honest. Once you have won their confidence and friendship, they will tell you what they think about anything in the world, whether they *know* anything about it or not. It is this free-and-easy attitude toward life that is so truly refreshing. Dull, dry facts mean nothing in their young existence. Convention has yet to cast its tight bonds around their minds or manners. They will cheerfully admit that they are smarter than their daddies, prettier than their mammas, and have a hundred sweethearts. They will guess about things they've never heard of before, and give advice about personal problems whose stormy thunderheads have never clouded their bright horizon. In short, they make the perfect interview—before an adult audience. But woe to the M.C. who tries to get laughs from an audience their own age. The discrepancies and "malaprops" are indistinguishable to such a group . . . and your show is dead. Grief, also, is in store for the smart-aleck M.C. who fails to win the kids' trust at the very outset, or who

pokes fun at them during any part of the show. No matter how absurd the answer, the man at the mike must either accept it as perfectly reasonable or laugh *with* the youngsters in a manner that shouts he is their friend.

In second place for interview honors, and almost in a dead heat for top spot, must come the old folks. Old ladies, in particular, with old gentlemen as acceptable substitutes. And when I say "old" I haven't any particular age in mind, but rather a period when the restrictions of life are tossed overboard and people begin to relax and say what they please. Tom Breneman found it when he began his "oldest lady" department on the "Breakfast in Hollywood" show. I discovered it when, years before, I awarded a bottle of champagne to the oldest guest at my "World's Fair Party." The reasons are essentially the same as those which apply to the youngsters. The fearful watch for propriety is gone; the worry about who is going to hear you say what is past. Old ladies gaily confess their youthful flirtations and reveal freely to millions of listening strangers exactly how they trailed and trapped their man. They, too, will give advice freely, but unlike the kiddies, their words are usually worth hearing because they've been around a long, long time and have outlived much of the nonsense that keeps the rest of us tied up in bundles of inhibitions. And if the M.C. gets too inquisitive, the oldster is not above giving him a smart verbal crack on the knuckles, to the huge delight of the listeners.

Of all the thousands I've interviewed on the air over the years, my favorite is still an eighty-five-year-old lady I know only as Madame X, who stepped up to my World's Fair microphone on Treasure Island one night and said she'd talk to me but her name was none of my business.

"If you must know, young man," she added tartly, "I come from an extremely well-known family in northern California who would be mortified beyond standing if they knew that I was making a spectacle of myself on the radio. If you want to ask me all these silly questions, you'll just have to call me Madame X!"

And with that we were off and away on the most enchanting conversation piece that I've ever helped put together. For everything I asked she had a quick and complete answer, and she spoke in a tone that left no room for doubt, gave no opportunity for rebuttal.

On modern women: "They gad around too much, leave their children alone too much, join too many clubs, and then nag their husbands when they can find any spare time to talk to him at all."

On modern men: "They're just like their fathers. Rascals! Every one of them a rogue you can't trust beyond rolling-pin range. But I wouldn't have them change for anything. If we women didn't have a man to worry about and try to reform, there'd be nothing to live for."

On the best years of a long life: "The last five! Since I've been eighty I can go out with anyone I like, go anywhere I please, and come home when I get ready, and nobody can ask any questions!"

On complaints: "Not a worry in the world. I'd only change two things if I could: first, I'd take the vote away from women and keep them out of things they don't know anything about. Second, I'd move my daughter over to the next county. She lives in the house next door, and when she hears me shutting the garage doors at 3 A.M. she sticks her head out the bedroom window and wants to know what I've been up to."

On the future: "I'll be spending a whole lot more time at home with my radio from now on. That's why I wanted to come over here and see what it's like to be on the working end of your gadget. The doctors tell me I'll be blind in a few months. I can't see well now. But don't give me any sympathy, young man. I've seen *plenty* in my lifetime. I've got pictures in my mind that'll do me if I live to be a thousand."

And, Madame X, *wherever* you are, and *whoever* you are . . . I hope you go right on living with the same zest for life that you crowded into my microphone that night. You're still the champ!

Good interviews can be found among people of all ages and all vocations. But the most difficult, generally, are among young housewives and old sea captains. There's a different reason for each group.

The young housewives are (with many, many exceptions) timid and fearful subjects. Between the ages of twenty and thirty they are on such uncertain ground, emotionally, mentally, and certainly domestically, that they hesitate to predict that the sun is coming up the next day. The extremely youthful ones are inclined to be giggly and almost hysterically self-

conscious, and the ones nearing their thirties are suspicious
and keenly aware of their new dignity. In brief, they are old
enough to know how little they have really experienced in
life, and yet they are young enough to feel embarrassed about
admitting it. Where their older sisters in the marriage sorority
are laughing about the first illusions they cherished, these be-
ginners are still wondering what it's all about and trying to
behave as if they knew. The resultant interviews are apt to
be monosyllabic and a strange mixture of anxiety and eagerness. That is why I almost invariably select a guest on the
basis of "volunteering," so that I am sure she really *wants*
to talk. Suddenly thrusting the mike into someone's face when
she least expects it is a poor way of insuring a good "spot."
On the other hand, when a "volunteer" suddenly gets mike
fright, the only way out of it is by gentle teasing. A kidding
accusation always breaks down the defenses and out comes
the real person, astride a white charger, intent on protecting
her honor.

"Tell me honestly now . . . do you ever read your husband's
letters or go through his pockets when he's asleep?" This
question, with a twinkle in the eye and an accusing waggle
of a finger, often does the trick.

"Oh NO! Of course not," she blurts out indignantly. "We
TRUST each other completely. Besides, he never keeps
money in his pants!"

By this time the crowd senses the byplay and is awaiting
the next question which will surely lead this righteous matron
to further claims that are a known fiction in the game of
marriage.

"Well, well, Mrs. Smith," comes the next lead, "that
sounds like a perfect marriage. How long have you been
wed, did you say?"

"Four years."

"And you've NEVER had a quarrel in that time?" Raised
eyebrows.

"Never ONCE!" Indignantly.

And away goes the audience for a twenty-second laugh.

This is not to say that many of my best interviews are not with the lovely ladies between twenty and thirty; but if anything in this uncertain business can be generalized, it is that young housewives are poor bets to interview unless they happen to be exceptions to the rule.

Sea captains are something else again. Take a young man, send him to sea, keep him aboard ships until well-seasoned, salt him down with the spray of ten thousand lonely nights on the flying bridge, isolate him with the stiff gold bars of a captaincy, and you have my nomination for the world's worst interview.

I have tried it a score of times. I've tried it in studios, on exposition grounds, and on the decks of ships. I've pleaded, prodded, and pressured them into broadcasts, only to have them explode in my face with a dull "pffft." Something happens to a man who is left alone too much. And when you talk to a captain of a freighter whose only conversation at sea is with equally taciturn officers, you have a man who hoards syllables like a ward heeler treasures votes. Even some of the captains of big ocean-going liners, whose jobs entail the entertaining of prominent passengers and who supposedly preside over the "captain's table" during the cruise, founder on the reefs of conversation when a mike is sighted dead ahead. Sometimes I think it's because they are really disdainful of talk; sometimes I think it's loyalty to the tradition of the "silent men" who go "down to the sea in ships"; and sometimes I think it's because they take a sadistic glee in watching a landlubber floundering in a Sargasso Sea of silence.

My last attempt was with a certain captain who commanded one of the largest liners in the United States Merchant Marine. His ship was making its maiden voyage up the West Coast from Los Angeles to San Francisco, and Warner Brothers decided to celebrate on board by staging the world première of the *Sea Wolf* starring Edward G.

Robinson and John Garfield. I went along with my trusty microphone and a ton of short-wave equipment to cover the proceedings. We arranged an ad-lib broadcast to take place from the main dining salon while en route up the coast. It turned out to be a rough and stormy night, with big, rolling swells giving the liner a motion much like a python going through jungle grass. By the time dinner was served, half of the "starlets," a third of the correspondents, and my engineer had all decided to make the trip "by rail." Eddie Robinson, the Sea Wolf, looked pretty green, and I was swallowing twice the number of times that is par for the entree. Garfield was having the time of his life, and the captain was quietly dining.

With fifteen minutes to go before broadcast time, my technician warned me to get ready for a voice test to the mainland. He assured me that the transmitter was throwing up a good signal. I told him it was about time . . . everyone else already had—I was glad it was the transmitter's turn. But somehow this didn't get much of a laugh from him.

We checked and double-checked the short-wave reception. I gathered the captain, Eddie Robinson, and Garfield for a final program huddle over the notes I had written. The anecdotes for the movie stars to tell were sure-fire, because they had been thoroughly "briefed" for their appearance by one of the smartest exploitation men in the business: Charlie Einfeld. But the captain was still dubious about my suggestions for *his* interview. From the publicity man of the line I had unearthed the stories of the captain's adventures in rescues at sea, shipwrecks, feats of heroism, and ultimately the Horatio Alger finale to a career that began as a cabin boy thirty years before. He nodded somewhat glumly as I raced over the details to refresh his memory, and then we were on the air.

Everything zipped along with the accustomed ease of a Hollywood première. Stars took their bows while the enthusiastic audience applauded. The producer, director, author, and assorted film folk reeled off their platitudes, while I beamingly herded them gently on and off the air. And then came the climax of the show. The captain spoke last, as the ranking official aboard, so it was upon him that the success of the broadcast would depend.

"Captain," I began hopefully, "you have a long and colorful record as a skipper and we'd like to recall some of the highlights for our listeners. How about the beginning: what happened that sent you to sea?"

"I needed a job."

"Yes?" I implored.

"That's all. I needed a job." He seemed quite pleased with the answer, and he was definitely ready for the next big, broad topic.

"Wonderful! Wonderful!" I pressed on. "And then as a cabin boy you started the long, slow climb to the top. Hasn't it been a great satisfaction to know that you gained your goal?"

"Yes."

"I knew you'd say that, Captain!" A small, hollow feeling began to undulate in the pit of my stomach. "The very tone of your voice bespeaks the determination that brought you to a captaincy of one of the world's greatest ships. Has it seemed a long climb?"

"Thirty years."

"How long was it actually, Captain?" I stalled while thinking.

"Thirty years."

The audience tittered as my thought processes stripped gears under the load. I sputtered.

"Thirty years! Well, well, thirty years!" My eyes lit on the item about the shipwreck and the rescue at sea. Here was my salvation! "The whole country has heard of your gallant rescue at sea in the Atlantic last winter. Won't you tell us about it, Captain?"

"No use, if the whole country has heard it."

"That was just a figure of speech, Captain. What I meant was that everybody has read the *headlines,* but we'd like to know the details as only you can give them . . . the dramatic, vivid, inside story of a rescue at sea!"

"Hmmmm," he grunted thoughtfully; then as he took in a deep breath, my spirits soared. At last he was going to thaw out and talk. "We sighted a ship in distress, hove to, transshipped their crew, and proceeded to port."

I felt like the albatross shot by the Ancient Mariner, except twice as dead. But I had to give it one last college try.

"What a thrilling story, Captain. And then the finale. Your ship arrives in your home port of Boston. The cheering crowds line the pier. Your family is there waiting to welcome the hero. How did you feel?"

"Fine."

The broadcast must have finished. Someone must have said the final good night and given the system cue. People said it was me. But I know differently; I was dead, buried, and gone to my just reward.

Making Love to Four Hundred People

How many times have you snuggled cozily by your set, enjoying your favorite comic, only to jerk to attention, puzzled, as the audience in the studio suddenly laughed uproariously at a very mediocre joke? And then I'll bet you asked yourself: "What's so funny about *that?*"

It happens all the time, and you can't be blamed for wondering if the ushers in the studios are instructed to inject some mysterious serum into people who attend broadcasts, in order to make them laugh loudly on signal.

Blame it on the "warm-up," which, after all, *is* a sort of serum injected into the audience before the broadcast to insure laughs on schedule! The audience is unaware of the treatment, of course, but it gets one just the same.

The "warm-up" is a period set aside to thaw the guests in the house, to put them in the proper frame of mind before the show. It is the most important part of the day's work for me and, I suspect, for most entertainers.

The performer also uses this "warm-up" period to put *himself* into the proper mood, as well as the audience. Perhaps he's just come from home and a scuffle with his mother-in-law and is decidedly not in a funny mood; or perhaps the tax collector has just paid him a visit, or his doctor has just told him those ulcers are getting serious. Obviously, under such conditions, he can't amble out on a cold stage, nod to his audience, and be a funny fellow; he's got to work himself into a pitch, forget his troubles, enjoy himself . . . or nobody will enjoy him. Thus the "warm-up."

The studio audience is necessary for the variety and comedy show, for it sets the pace for the entertainer. How difficult it would be for Jack Benny to tell a joke if nobody laughed! His timing would be off completely. It could be the funniest joke ever told, but if you sat at home and heard no laughs following it, you'd subconsciously say to yourself: "I guess it isn't funny!" and switch to another station. But when you hear the joke, followed by a tremendous "boff" from the studio audience, your subconscious automatically suggests you laugh too; you enjoy Jack Benny's program.

So it is important for the comedian or master of ceremonies to make sure, before he goes on the air, that the studio audience *is* in the proper receptive frame of mind.

Audiences are amazing. Each group of four hundred persons has a separate mob personality. A great many things affect them collectively: If it is raining outside, they are glum and need an extra push; if it is a nice day, their spirits are high; if it is a Friday night, they're usually in a holiday mood; Monday audiences are slow and many times "dare you to make them laugh!"

Often there is one person in the crowd of four hundred who has a nice loud and infectious laugh. That one person can lead the rest into being good spectators, willing and ready. He's a bellwether who starts off in the right direction, and the rest follow happily. I don't mean to imply that such a bellwether is employed by comedians or entertainers; we all just hope he shows up, and many like him!

An experienced showman can tell what sort of audience he has to deal with five seconds after he's on the stage. They may look exactly alike; it may be the same hour of the same day of the week; and they may be from the same neighborhood . . . yet each broadcast brings together a combination of strangers that might be hot, lukewarm, or cold. I can't tell you what makes the difference, but it's there.

Even before I open my mouth to say "hello," I can tell pretty well what I'm up against; I have the "feel" of the folks down front. I sense the friendliness of the applause, the way they look me over as I step to the center of the stage. The volume of applause may sound the same every day to the unpracticed ear, but as the years go by, the performer feels the shadings of enthusiasm in the quick way the bulk of the applause gathers momentum, in the sustained quality of the sound, and in the prolonged fullness of it. Next time you attend a stage show or a night club, watch the applause; you'll see what I mean. It may be dutiful, begrudging, lackadaisical, or spontaneous.

To discover quickly which kind of an audience I am facing, I make my first comment and wait for the backlash. An experienced entertainer learns to develop an opening remark that is "sure-fire." It brings a definite, measurable response. If the audience is a "dream" audience, the opening remark at once sets off an explosion of welcome laughter. If it is a normal, healthy audience, a nice round laugh will be the reaction. If it is a "dead" audience, I'll hear a titter here and there, a few strained, forced laughs, and the rest is stony silence. Thus, from the opening remark, the master of ceremonies is able to tell how hard he's going to have to work that day.

My job is about to begin; the "warm-up" is about to start.

I have collected half a dozen guaranteed, sure-fire, time-tested, dyed-in-the-wool, double-strength, bona-fide gags which never fail to produce some sort of excitement in the crowd. Each is stronger than its predecessor until a peak is reached. How many I use and how far I go depends on the folks out front.

Once the crowd is with me and in the mood for nonsense, the serious business of actually selecting the "volunteers" gets under way. And no matter how much *fun* it appears to the spectator, it actually is a *serious* matter, since a "dud" contestant can sometimes sink a whole show . . . especially if he's an opening guest.

One popular method for picking the people is to "take a chance" and wait until the show actually is on the air. This is the most dangerous of all schemes, but it adds the most spice to the show and keeps the M.C. on his guard. It's not really such a chance as the uninitiated might think, for it is used only where the show is a fast-moving, variety-audience show in the aisles of the studio; no single guest or stunt is so important that you are "stuck" with it. I employ this "catch-as-catch-can" system on my "House Party" show every afternoon, and if I run across a dull and stodgy contestant, I'm off and away in a flash before the show bogs down. Then, too, during the quarter-hour "warm-up" I've been busy watching the reactions of individuals scattered through the audience. When I spot someone with a hearty laugh and a twinkle in her eye, I mentally mark that seat for a "visit" when we go on the air. Oh yes, I've been fooled plenty of times . . . but that's part of the fun for me, and if I'm having fun, the show is certain to reflect it.

On "People Are Funny" it is vitally important to have only the very choice cuts of contestant. To begin with, there are only three and sometimes four stunts in the entire half hour. Each guest has to carry the ball for a long and complicated run. Spoilsports, Fearful Freddies, and overdeveloped "life-of-the-party" boys would kill the show in a minute, because whomever we have, we're stuck with him for at least ten minutes. Thus the "warm-up" for "People Are Funny" is perhaps the longest and most arduous in all of broadcasting. It is a complete show in itself and lasts for a full thirty to thirty-five minutes. This too can be dangerous, because the pre-show fun can be so hilarious and visual that the actual show can turn out to be an anticlimax. (Red Skelton, for instance, has to "tone down" his pre-broadcast antics and present most of his "extra" fun AFTER the broadcast, because his clowning is so full of screams that the gags on the show are pale by comparison.)

After the preliminary routine of stories and gags and get-acquainted gimmicks, I frankly confess to my audience that the whole show depends on the volunteers we have, and that we never pick anyone who doesn't WANT to have fun and isn't ANXIOUS to be on the air. Then, depending upon the requirements of the script for that night, I pick THREE volunteers for each ONE needed for the actual broadcast. I may ask for three married civilian men between the ages of twenty-five and forty. Or I may ask for three single women over forty. It might be married couples who have been wed for a certain number of years or who come from a special part of the United States originally. Whatever it is, I pick at least three from which one will be finally selected to prove that "People Are Funny."

Then I put each of the three volunteers for the spot through a "test" which involves his ability to talk, think, and use his imagination. It might be a quick one-minute interview with each one pretending he is someone else: an explorer, a big-game hunter, a prize fighter, a crook, or a midget in a circus. It might be a thirty-second "speech" on some inane subject such as how to make a baby stop crying, or how to knit an afghan. It might be a "salesmanship" test with me being the housewife and the guest trying to sell me an object that I mention on the spot, such as a cow, a girdle, or a mustache cup. After each of the three has been given a test in the same category of stunts, the audience applause decides which one it wants to have on the show. The losers are thanked and handed consolation prizes.

The amazing part of this scheme is that the studio audience invariably selects the best contestant by its applause. Not once in a hundred times am I surprised by the final choice. This is borne out by the high percentage of "hits" on the actual broadcast.

There is a lot more than "chance" to account for this uncanny audience selection. I have been careful to keep the hearers impartial by detouring their prejudices in matters of home town, vocation, need, and name. The actual names and whereabouts of the volunteers are never known until they are announced on the program. If, for instance, I discovered in the "warm-up" that one of the guests was a carpenter with five children from Pennsylvania and that he had been in the infantry overseas . . . no matter how he performed he would get the applause of (1) men in the construction business, (2) mothers who have or want large families, (3) everybody from Pennsylvania, (4) everybody who had been in the infantry or had a friend or relative in the infantry. Without this knowledge, the crowd can be counted on to applaud fairly.

This sort of selection automatically eliminates the undesirables. The smart aleck hasn't a prayer. Recently one of these "hep" characters stepped up to the mike, took out a wad of gum, stuck it under the microphone, and said, "What's the sixty-four-dollar question, Bud?" I knew the answer before we went a syllable further: he was a dead pigeon.

The brash, impudent contestant is no better off. An easy familiarity with me, the microphone, or the audience spells his doom.

And the eccentrics, drunks, and "professional" contestants are eliminated by my handling of their "subject" in the warm-up tests. I select something that guarantees their automatic disappearance. The "eccentrics" are the hardest to detect because they are only slightly daffy, and as such they're difficult to segregate from slightly nervous but otherwise perfectly honest extroverted volunteers. Give them a test to make up a story, though, and they'll make it so wildly surrealistic the audience suspects they're professionals and shies away.

The dangerous "drunks" are not really stiff, just high enough to be floating around on Cloud 9, completely uninhibited and ready for a hell of a time with anybody. This is perilous; a man slightly tipsy can win the affections of a crowd by the sheer frankness of his answers. If this is happening, I give him a ticket to next week's show, thank him for trying, and tell him to come back as my guest on the following Friday and try again when he hasn't had a few drinks. "This," I explain, "is an NBC ruling and I'm awfully sorry, but that's the way it has to be."

The true "professional" contestant is something else again: mostly women who have plenty of time on their hands and who somehow get their hands on tickets to every quiz and audience show. They are the sour pickle in my scoop of vanilla. They lie in your face when you ask them if they haven't been on before. They yell out answers when you're on the air. And they have a reinforced steel nerve that the atom bomb couldn't budge. They are willing to submit to any indignity, perform any stunt, or try to answer any question if there's a prize in it. Some masters of ceremonies actually like to have them in the audience as a sure-fire "act" to fall back on when the going gets rough. I do not like them because they are not doing it for fun, and I will not tolerate them on my shows because I feel they are depriving someone of honest sport and a worth-while prize. Most of them in Hollywood have long since stopped volunteering on my shows because I have a long memory for faces and the word has gone out that "Linkletter won't give you a chance!" If they're smart enough to get tickets by some devious way, they are welcome enough to occupy a seat, but I make it very clear in my opening remarks that anyone who's been on before is "kaput."

There's a great difference between Eastern and Western "professional" contestants. First, there are three to five times as many per show in New York, which is understandable when you compare populations. And more important, the Eastern boys and girls make an organized racket of it. They come to the studios with World Almanacs, encyclopedias, and notebooks filled with cross-indexed information about everything from asafetida to zzerbias. Many of the programs use a device in which every guest is invited to guess the number of languages in the world, the distance to the moon, the height of the Washington Monument, or anything else obscure and open to wild guessing. At the close of the show

the one closest gets a big prize. This kind of show is meat and drink for these walking "libraries," and they will hit the most remote topic right on the nose. One producer I know clipped a tiny "filler" out of a small weekly which listed the tonnage of beef shipped out of the Argentine in the first six months of 1945. He knew that figure would not appear in any almanac for at least a year, and he filed the "clipping" safely for a few months and then sprung it on one of his shows. Midway in the program a beaming, white-haired lady "happened" to hit the right number to the very final digit!

In Hollywood the so-called "professional" is more apt to be a bored housewife who haunts the networks in hopes of occasional prizes that she'll win whether she knows anything or not. There is not the "organization" back of the

Western regular. And there is not the newest kind of pest that you hear so often from New York: the "professional Brooklynite." This type of character either deliberately misunderstands, misquotes, or shows off by ignorant behavior, and is gradually becoming one of the more obnoxious fixtures. I do not believe they do the regular citizens of Brooklyn any good. The so-called "Quiz Queen," Mrs. Sadie Hertz, is my nomination for the Number One guest to be kept off the air by my colleagues in the East, in spite of her sure-fire exhibitionism. *People* are funny enough!

There is one more important consideration in the selection and preparation of a guest for a broadcast like "People Are Funny." After he has won a spot on the show in competition with other guests, the producers must make sure he STAYS the way he was in his pre-broadcast performance. A subtle psychological change often occurs during those few minutes that elapse between the elimination and the air show. Mr. Shoe Clerk thinks to himself: "Well, for heaven's sake, I guess I'm a pretty funny guy, after all, to win a place on the show. I never realized before that I must be a born showman. Probably missed my calling. But now that I *know*, I'm really going to turn it on when we hit the air. I'll murder 'em."

This sort of stream of consciousness is a good cross section of many contestants' thinking, and we have learned to give each of them a small warning talk before going into the actual show. We tell them that the reason the audience chose them was because of their unaffected enthusiasm and straightforward attempts to please, and if they want the whole nation to have the same good opinion, they should let US make the funnies, while THEY behave as normally and naturally as possible. At the same time we also caution them about the various taboos on the radio, have them sign a standard form releasing us of responsibility in case of an accident, and in some cases make sure that their health is O.K. for a particularly arduous stunt.

When the half hour is over, everything that can possibly be done to insure a good unrehearsed show has been checked. The sifting and screening has given us normally intelligent, extroverted people who are not wise guys or scaredy-cats. The studio audience has been kidded, prodded, tickled, and teased; I'm keyed up to a fast pace and have the confidence necessary to a good performance. Then when that red light flashes on and the one hundred and forty-five stations of the National Broadcasting Company join us in Hollywood, everybody is in the act. The "warm-up" is over and we're "On the Air!"

People Are Still Funny

A TIMID LITTLE MAN IN A GREAT BROWN COAT SIDLED UP to a shelf of books in the quiet sanctuary of the Hollywood Branch Public Library.

Guiltily he cast a nervous glance about him and slyly he removed a book from beneath his coat. Again he looked about him. Then he placed the book on the shelf.

His movements went unobserved by an elderly gentleman peering over his glasses at the day's newspaper. A college girl, reference volumes spread before her, moistened her pencil thoughtfully and made some marks in her notebook. There was a great silence in the brightly lighted room.

Again the timid little man in the great brown coat looked about him, saw nothing to fear, cleared his throat, and removed his book from the shelf!

Although no one in the library saw or cared what he was doing, this little man was the object of wonder in millions of homes throughout America. His every movement was of gnawing interest to a great audience. He was a "People Are Funny" contestant and he was merely following my instructions.

When he had removed his book from the shelf, he casually strolled over to a table, sat down, opened his book, and began to read. When he had finished the first page, he calmly reached up, took a firm grip, and *tore the page out of the book noisily!* He noisily crumpled it and threw it on the floor. Then he turned his attention to the next page, carefully read it, and calmly tore it out too!

Curious eyes rose from the tops of books in every corner of the reading room. But the sound of ripping pages was the only noise to be heard.

The timid little man tore out the third page. And the fourth page. And the fifth page. Carefully he read each one and calmly he tore it from the binding and threw it on the floor.

Still following instructions, he increased his pace. He reached page twenty. By this time heads were together and whispers echoed midst the books on the shelves. There was a sharp clack-clack-clack of high female shoes. The librarian had noticed something amiss from her sanctuary behind the desk and was arriving for an investigation.

A sharp glance from the little man notified him of the librarian's approach. He switched his tactics, half rose from his chair in righteous wrath, began pulling bunches of pages from his book and throwing them in the air in a frenzy.

"This book's no darn good!" he screamed. And he tore out another bunch of pages. "And I've read it before anyway!" And another sheaf of pages swirled in the air.

We had told our contestant to do exactly what he had done. We told him there was nothing to fear, inasmuch as it was our book, and we had given it to him to smuggle into the library. What we had *neglected* to tell him was that inside the back cover was stamped: "Property of the Los Angeles Public Library. Misuse of this book in any way is a misdemeanor and the violator is subject to fines or imprisonment or both." We knew it was there because we had put it there ourselves!

Well, the librarian made quite a fuss over the way the little guy was wrecking her library.

"Oh, it's all right," he loftily explained. "I brought this book in here myself. It's mine. I can do anything I want with it."

While the contestant looked on, the librarian took the

remains of the volume, thumbed through the pages, and looked at the inside of the back cover.

"*Your* book?" Her eyebrows arched as she pointed to the stamp on the back page. "Did you say this was *your* book?"

The timid little man looked at the horrible spot where the end of her finger rested. He gulped. He stammered an idiotic apology. And he mentioned the name "Art Linkletter" profanely.

The librarian selected two youthful men from the dozen spectators who by now had collected at the table. "If you gentlemen will watch this madman, I'll call the police."

The contestant was frightened by this time. He'd figured he was safe as long as he tore up his own book. But this was something different. This was somebody else's book!

The Hollywood Police Station is but a short block from the library, and it took about ten seconds for the cops to enter the door. Gruffly they inquired of the librarian about the trouble. She told them everything.

With the end of her tale, the police grabbed our man. Each took an arm. Protesting violently, pleading, arguing, explaining, demanding, insisting, swearing, he was hauled off.

Then our man Atkins stepped out from behind a bush and took over. The police, of course, were in on the whole deal. They came back to the program, bringing the contestant with them. He was a pretty mad contestant, too, as I recall.

Well, we wanted to find out what would happen if somebody disturbed the silence of a public library with a really eccentric plan. And we found out. We're very scientific on "People Are Funny." We're always trying to find out things!

Naturally we ended the stunt, after the contestant had recited all the details, with a lengthy and sincere appeal to save books and to patronize public libraries.

Unfortunately, we never can obtain all of the details of what happens when we pull an outside stunt like that one, but it is fun to speculate on what probably happened. For instance, I'll bet that night in at least a dozen Los Angeles homes people were saying: "I was down at the library tonight, dear, and the darnedest thing happened. A guy came in and started tearing pages out of a book and . . ."

One of the most successful "outside" stunts first began with a rather simple but devastating alterations trip to a big department store. We had dressed our contestant in the clothes of a foreman of a building crew. We hired a gang of genuine construction men to accompany him. And he, the contestant himself, was to lead them into the busy main floor of the Broadway Hollywood Department Store and direct them in setting up transits, levels, lead lines, and other paraphernalia necessary to extensive remodeling. Oblivious of clerks, floorwalkers, or other store executives, he was to shout to his men: "Right here we'll put up the new wall for the soda fountain! Over here get your markings for the elevator shaft to go through! We'll have to tear out this entire column for the new archway!"

No matter who came up to him or what they said, he was to keep his gang busy marking Xs on the floors, and if any official became too insistent, he was to look blankly and say, "I don't know what it's all about. I just take my orders from the owners."

The volunteer picked for this lovely detail was a schoolteacher on vacation from Portland, Oregon, and I'll bet he's never lived that night down with the kids in his classes. He'll be known as the "Big Wreck" the rest of his days.

He did precisely as instructed, and the store management went wild. The floorwalker called the department head. That worthy called the superintendent. He checked with the general manager. And after a futile visit with our "wrecker," the manager started calling the owners who were scattered from Kansas City to San Diego.

The stunt worked so beautifully and created so much

general havoc that we decided to refine it for future use.

On the next time out, a few months later, we had selected a private home for the "Operation Blasting." As before, an innocent guest was selected at random from the studio audience, dressed like a foreman, and sent with his crew of professional surveyors and engineers to the home which we had prepicked because the repairman of a local radio shop had assured us that he was fixing the only radio set that this particular family owned. We knew that they would not be able to hear what was being plotted and thus ruin the gag.

The fake gang of builders rolled up to the house in their truck. They set up transits on the lawn. They yelled about "blasting right here" and "steam shovel over there" until half the neighborhood was out watching and wondering. Finally the "foreman" couldn't stand the suspense any longer and he went up to ring the doorbell. A startled housewife opened the door and soon the man of the house came rushing out to demand what was going on here, anyway.

Our contestant calmly told him that they were from the Los Angeles Freeway Construction Department and would he please sign this paper condemning his home so they could get busy and start blasting. He concluded with the matter-of-fact words:

"The new highway will go right about through the northwest corner of your living room. You ought to feel mighty proud, sir."

By this time our Mr. Atkins, from a distance of fifty feet, could see the blood pressure beginning to shoot steam out of the householder's ears, and he came on the run to explain the gag and bring them all back to NBC.

Actually the last laugh was on us, because the Freeway Association had BEEN through that very neighborhood the week before with news of the impending highway. And, as the family told us on the air:

"We thought something was awfully funny, because the

city planners never moved that fast on anything before in their lives . . . so why *now?*"

Still another satanic form taken by this particular stunt occurred a few months later when three volunteers went out as a crew of paperhangers to a rented home with fake orders from the owner to start redecorating the interior of the living room. They were given big rolls of outlandish wallpaper, buckets of paste, and big brushes with which to slosh on the glue. When they admitted that they hadn't the slightest idea how to hang wallpaper, I told them not to worry about details, but to cover everything from the ceiling down. This was to be a rush job; no pictures were to be taken down or fixtures removed . . . "just cover 'em up and let 'em bump out."

When this enthusiastic gang of house wreckers finally returned with their fuming victims in tow we had a terrific time mollifying the wife. She had invited relatives in for a bridge party that night, and her walls were now festooned with repulsive strips of red and yellow paper, while paste was dripping from the chandelier where one of our amateur paperhangers had fallen, bucket and all, from a stepladder.

It took a three-hundred-dollar radio, a set of sterling silver, and a promise of a complete new decoration job to get us off the hook on that one.

Probably for sheer, unmitigated nerve, the topper for these "gang" visits came when we sent out a dozen different contestants, all dressed up in screwball costumes, to call on a certain unsuspecting family and announce that they had come for the big party. Engraved cards with the victim's name and address had been prepared in advance, and the counterfeit "guests" arrived singly, in pairs, and quartets with much shouting, waving of party favors, and effusive thanks to the bewildered host and hostess for the invitations. They trooped right into the living room, went back to the kitchen, and started raiding the icebox, and finally, when the completely befuddled householder started to telephone for the police, he was told the party would all adjourn to NBC for the pay-off on "People Are Funny."

There's a streak of perverse human nature in all of us, I guess. That's why millions of listeners stay home on Friday nights to watch our show. They are entertained, first of all. And amused. But whether they'll admit it to themselves or not, they still receive a vicarious thrill from the exploits of our contestants. It isn't very hard to picture yourself in such a spot.

Perhaps you'll remember the time we dressed a woman in a wedding outfit and sent her out on Hollywood Boulevard to look for her groom, who had supposedly vanished. She had a bedraggled bunch of flowers, a torn veil, and a sorrowful look as she hurried off to inquire in each store, restaurant, or bar, "Have you seen Henry? He ran off right after he said 'I do' and I thought I saw him come in here." That night countless women shuddered in vicarious fright and an equal number of husbands hid smiles of suppressed delight from their sharp-eyed spouses.

It's this same streak of perverse human nature that sends millions of dialers to CBS when Red Skelton is a "mean widdle kid." During the time he's smashing furniture, kicking his friends, and defying every rule, grownups everywhere are grinning in pure glee as they recall their own childhood misadventures.

I don't mean to imply that the secret of our success is to smash things right and left. That is only *one* ingredient in the formula for proving that people are funny.

The others run the gamut of human experience: fibbing, bragging, flirting, winning, losing, and gambling are just a few of the other items on our long list. The more universal the fault we point out, the more amusing it is to people. For instance, if we picked a volunteer and dressed him like

an insane-asylum patient and sent him out to look for an imaginary dog named "Napoleon" (which we did), it would be mildly amusing to most listeners but it would lack the very important element of common experience. After all, very few of us have ever been in that kind of a spot ourselves, nor have we often met anyone in that condition. But, on the other hand, if we dressed a man in a soaking-wet overcoat and hat, loaded him down with bundles, popcorn, peanuts, candy, and a dripping umbrella, and then sent him to a theater where he would bumble his way through crowded rows in search of a seat—then almost everyone in our entire listening audience would sit back, nod his head in agreement, and say to anyone within earshot, "That's just like the dope who stepped all over my feet last week at the Bijou, doggone it!"

Our most difficult task is convincing the listeners that we really DO send our volunteers out to accomplish the jobs we've assigned them. I suppose that it *is* hard to believe that anyone in his right mind would actually offer (and even fight for the chance) to do the insane things we dream up, but I've seen it happen for so many years that it no longer surprises me when lawyers, doctors, drug clerks, mothers, and plumbers mob me when I ask for someone to go out and lead a conga line up the middle of Vine Street.

Just as a little convincer, however, we advertise a standing offer of ten thousand dollars cash to anyone who can prove that our contestants are not sent out to the places we say they go and attempt to do the stunts you hear me tell about on the air.

Even the stars in the business find it hard to believe that we go through with everything. I'll never forget the night Eddie Cantor was to go out to a nearby neighborhood with a lady contestant, where they were to go from door to door ringing bells and asking for contributions of waste fat for the government. It was actually Eddie Cantor, but the lady volunteer was told he was Eddie's *stand-in,* and her job was to try to convince the folks in the homes called on that it was really Cantor. When she finally came back with Eddie, she laughed and laughed as she told us how she fooled all of the poor dopes and how they thought it was Cantor. You should have seen her face when I told her that it HAD been Banjo-Eyes all the time! But what I started out to say was that after I had explained what they were to do and sent the pair of them off-stage, Cantor blandly asked our assistant which dressing room they sat down to wait in until it was time to go back on the air. When he was told that they DIDN'T sit anywhere, but they really WENT out to do the job, Eddie was flabbergasted. Of course he went right along with the gag and did a wonderful job both inside AND outside!

This "outside stunt" is perhaps the outstanding characteristic of the "People Are Funny" show. Almost everyone in America knows about the dirty double crosses that have been engineered on unsuspecting contestants, householders, bartenders, hotel clerks, businessmen, and even Hollywood policemen. Sometimes the contestant thinks he's on the "inside" of a practical joke, only to wake up and discover he's definitely out on the limb himself. Other times the people who live in private residences within a few miles of our studios get the "business" as our volunteers descend upon them in bunches as large as fifteen or twenty at a time. Very few restaurants, hotels, or private businesses in the vicinity of Hollywood and Vine have not been visited by our little demon participants in the last nineteen years.

The real secret behind the success of this stunt is the suspense which is created at the very start of the show and does not pay off until the last three minutes. Thousands of letters attest to the fact that listeners have been on their way to dinner, business engagements, or home when something intriguing was begun at the beginning of the program, and they were stuck to their sets and late for their dates because they HAD to find out what happened to the poor victim of our diabolical machinations.

Many listeners want to know why we don't let them actually listen in on the stunt as it develops outside the studio. Most people know that "remote-control" equipment is used on many shows to bring events to the air which cannot be created inside the network headquarters. But we have found that the old saying "Anticipation is greater than realization" applies with double force to our program. When we send a man out with a skunk on the end of a cord, nothing can possibly happen to that man on the crowded boulevards as funny as the images conjured up by the listener in his own mind. And then, too, most of our stunts are predicated on the complete innocence of the bystander, and this would be impossible with engineers running helter-skelter around the place carrying wires, microphones, and portable equipment. It is virtually impossible to conceal the fact that you are broadcasting from a spot because of the advance work needed to run in telephone lines and hook up various intercommunication systems.

Like almost every other department of the show, our "outside" stunt developed from an experimental try early in the series. On the very first show we wondered how suspicious people would be of a stranger approaching them on the street and offering them money. So we picked out a contestant, loaded him down with silver dollars, and instructed him to walk up to people and say, "I beg your pardon, but would you accept a dollar?"

Twenty minutes later he came back to report that only three people had taken a dollar. The other thirty people he had accosted had pushed him off with muttered explanations: "I'm sorry, but I'm too busy to stop."

The audience was hysterical over that simple demonstration, and even before the volunteer returned, I could detect a suspenseful atmosphere throughout the studio as they waited to see the outcome. We incorporated this experimental kind of stunt as a permanent opening and close for the show, and since then I've been just as curious each week as the listener to discover what really happened.

Some of our present-day stunts are highly complicated, expensive pieces of business that in no way resemble the simple little devices of 1941. For instance, last summer we sent a young honeymooning couple by airplane to the wilderness of Oregon to live for three weeks in a covered wagon, cook over an open fire, and otherwise live as their pioneer forefathers did one hundred years ago. For added spice, there was a treasure hunt for a thousand dollars. After three weeks of truly rough "outdoor" living they finally found the thousand in the lap of screen-star Susan Hayward, who was sitting in the front row of the studio audience back in Hollywood. That stunt took a great deal of careful planning. We even sent one of our agents to Oregon weeks in advance, to make sure the honeymooners really would live as "pioneers."

There was ample suspense in a situation we planned one night in which a young lady was involved up to her neck. Perhaps you remember it.

A few days before the broadcast we inserted a classified advertisement in the Hollywood *Citizen-News*. The ad, placed in the personal column, read:

WANTED: Adventurous men looking for unusual business opportunity. Be in the lobby of the Hollywood Plaza Hotel at 6 P.M. Friday. Wear a white carnation in your lapel and look for a beautiful brunette girl carrying a red rose.

The ad appeared in the paper just once. In our program meeting the week before, we had argued back and forth for several hours over the luck we'd have with that ad. The general consensus was pessimistic: nobody would answer it. But I pointed out that even if nobody did answer the ad, the test would be interesting. After all, the ad did carry plenty of allure and mystery, and certainly Hollywood, of all places, ought to be able to provide plenty of adventurous men. We decided to leave it to fate.

That Friday night I selected a lovely brunette from the studio audience, interviewed her briefly, gave her a red rose, and then asked her to read the advertisement in the paper. As the idea dawned on her and the audience, a ripple of excitement ran through the studio. What *would* happen? None of us knew. We said good-by to her and sent her on her way.

Twenty minutes later the doors to the studio banged open and in she came . . . followed by a laughing, noisy mob of two hundred men, all wearing white carnations! They were old and young, fat and thin, civilians, soldiers, sailors, marines, war workers, and they all looked as if they felt a trifle silly.

From the breathless story our lovely brunette gasped into the microphone, we learned that this carnation-wearing mob had been milling in front of the Plaza Hotel for more than half an hour and had been joined by another curious hundred without carnations. They filled the lobby, the bar, the restaurant and spilled out into the street where traffic was tied up for an hour.

It seems that she never even got into the hotel lobby. The waiting mob came howling down on her, swept her off her feet, and demanded to know where they were going. She yelled "NBC" and the mob took off. When it arrived a block down Vine Street, outside the gates of the network building, the guards were paralyzed with confusion, and before they could raise a halting hand the mob had boiled inside. Following the almost hysterical brunette, they conga'd through the double studio doors of our broadcasting room and onto the stage where I stood goggle-eyed with surprise. The studio audience went wild.

When peace finally descended, I explained to our listeners what had happened, interviewed the girl on her experiences, awarded her a handsome phonograph-radio combination, and then faced the two hundred men.

Originally we had figured if somebody *did* show up looking for an unusual business opportunity, we'd have one: a job at Douglas Aircraft in Santa Monica. To that end we had fortunately invited the personnel director of Douglas to be on the show that night. Luck was with us, for Douglas needed more than two hundred men to build their big transport planes for the Army. We offered the jobs to the two hundred and I later learned fifty of them accepted and went to work. People were *unusually* funny that night.

A much more complicated "outside" stunt, involving advance research and detective work that would make Philo Vance blink unbelievingly, was the frame-up on a returned soldier. We knew, of course, that all servicemen had at some time or another told their buddies, "If you ever get out my way, back home in the good old U.S.A., be sure to look me up and say hello. There'll always be a spot there for you if you get stuck, old pal. Let's have another quick one before hitting the sack."

With the help of a conniving buddy, we found out all about a certain ex-sergeant of the infantry, back from Philippines duty, and now living with his wife and youngster in a tiny rented cottage within a half mile of NBC. Checking further through relatives, employers, and schoolteachers, we assembled a mass of data about where he'd been to school, what he'd done in business, and some of his favorite pastimes.

Then, picking a married couple out of our studio audience, we armed them with this intimate file of information, loaded them down with suitcases, bird cages, and large, scratching dogs on leashes and sent them forth to take up good old "Charley" on his long-since-forgotten offer of hospitality.

I would have given anything to have been lying beneath the porch when that little drama unfolded. We couldn't possibly have smuggled engineers, wires, equipment, and microphones undetected into a spot where the dialogue could have been picked up for our radio audience. And considering what the ex-sergeant finally said when he learned of the hoax, it was just as well. We'd have been off the air for the night.

It turned out that he was one of the best sports ever to appear on the program. He was still laughing when we put the mike before him, and his wife could hardly talk as the enormity of the hoax sent laugh tears streaming down her cheeks. They had one tiny bedroom for themselves. Their six-year-old boy slept on the couch in the living room. They were expecting a visit from her mother that week end, and here was an old "buddy" of his, with a wife and a ton of baggage, demanding to be taken in for just "a few weeks or months."

The blowoff had been the final quiet statement of the visiting "buddy's" wife, when she twisted her hands pitifully, dabbed at her eyes, and said, "I know you *really* don't want us, in spite of all your excuses, and I wouldn't mind if it were just Randy and myself. But . . . well . . . you see, I'm expecting a little one soon."

With this, the little bungalow had been thrown open for them to stay as long as they liked. The youngster was to be moved out to the garage, the "infanticipator" was to be given the master bed, and the poor ex-sergeant and his wife would share the living-room furniture in makeshift fashion until "something else turned up."

The way that couple came through made your heart sing. In the dead, cyclone center of this tornado of laughs the warm, unselfish spirit of this veteran and his family stood as a real tribute to the comradeship that comes out of a war.

We gave him everything but the National Broadcasting Company.

And we gave a lot of returned soldiers, listening in, the cold shivers, as they prodded memories to try to remember their own carefree promises of "room and board any time you get by our house!"

The one stunt during the war period that we honestly expected to bring angry reactions from law-abiding, war-fighting citizens failed miserably. It had to do with stealing gasoline.

With gasoline rationed and difficult to obtain, we wondered one day at a writers' meeting just what would happen if we went out and swiped some . . . in full view of police and public. So we tried it.

Our victim in this case was a Hollywood playwright. We never know who'll volunteer! He seemed game for anything.

We dressed him in shabby clothing, gave him a five-gallon can, a length of rubber hose, and instructed him to go up busy Vine Street at the height of evening traffic. We further instructed him to begin at the end of a line of parked automobiles and work his way up the line, siphoning a drop or two from each tank he passed.

Just to make it easy for pedestrians, and there were hundreds of them, to report to the authorities, we stationed a policeman in plain sight up the street. We didn't expect anyone to scream "Thief!" but we did expect at least two or three persons to sidle up to the officer and whisper that something was amiss. We planned to take such informers into custody, bring them back to the studio, and reward their alertness and sense of duty by giving them fifty dollars in cash.

Not one soul reported what hundreds witnessed: the theft in broad daylight of gasoline from parked cars!

Even a police patrol car passed by slowly and didn't interfere.

After eight or nine cars had been canvassed, a sedan halted beside the "thief." The driver leaned from his window and shouted:

"What're ya doin', buddy?"

Our "thief" replied, "I'm stealing some gas so I can get to El Monte tonight!"

Why he said "El Monte" no one will ever know. It is a

small suburb about twenty miles east of Los Angeles. At any rate, the driver of the sedan became disgusted.

"If you need gas that bad, I'll *drive* you to El Monte," he muttered, and opened the door.

At this point our "outside man," Irv Atkins, virtually collapsed, when he saw our contestant actually climb in beside the driver of a strange car and disappear around a corner!

Cursing, Irv hurried back to the show, dreaming up explanations about how he'd lost a volunteer. As he puffed onto the stage, there, talking to me, was the "thief." He'd accepted a ride . . . as far as the studio!

"You, sir," I casually informed a husky young mechanic who had volunteered one Friday night, "have missed your question, so we can't give you the hundred-dollar bill we promised." He smiled a disappointed grin but wanted me to know he was a good sport anyway. After the proper pause I went on:

"But we're pretty decent around here about things like this. We'll give you another chance to earn that hundred. Okay?"

He gulped and smiled again. It was okay with him. I think he'd have dived off the Santa Monica pier with an anchor around his neck if I'd asked him in that moment of his gratefulness for another chance and, I might add, he would have been better off if he had taken the anchor.

"Are you a football fan?"

He nodded.

"Ever get excited at a big game and have an awful feeling that you'd like to rush out on the field and tackle somebody?"

He shook his head at this one.

"Well, I've had that feeling. And I've often wondered just what would happen if a spectator *did* succumb to his baser instincts and butt into a game. And tonight, right after the show, we're going to find out once and for all. YOU, Mr. Blank, are going to perform the experiment!"

There was terror on the contestant's face and cold sweat on his brow. But he nodded assent and the stunt was on.

At eight-thirty that night the John Guedels, the Art Linkletters, and the mechanic and his wife occupied a box on the fifty-yard line at the Los Angeles Coliseum game between the University of California at Los Angeles and St. Mary's Pre-Flight Service School. Many of the latter team were former All-American college stars, and the U.C.L.A. eleven was a championship team that year. The stands were loaded with fifty or sixty thousand rabid rooters.

Our instructions to the mechanic were that he was to suddenly rush out on the field and tackle the man carrying the ball. He could choose his time and victim.

I was as nervous as the contestant, for this was the first time I had ever been this close to one of our screwy outside stunts. In all other stunts I'd been safely busy in the studio, surrounded by friends and people I knew. But this time I was in on it too. There was no protection in case something went wrong. I didn't know if the combined rooting sections would rise in wrath and tar and feather the mechanic and the Guedels and the Linkletters before the night was over.

Evidently the same thoughts were running through the mechanic's head, for he allowed numerous opportunities for his tackle to escape. Frequently he'd renew his courage from a bottle of rye he'd tucked into his coat pocket. I began to think he was never going to attempt what might be his last act on earth.

As time wore on and my nerves wore out, I decided we'd better take some protective measures. The crowd looked too large to handle in case of a riot when our man made his tackle. I talked it over with John and he agreed. He was as nervous as I. So we hailed a couple of policemen and let them in on the secret. They nodded sagely, although I discovered later they didn't believe us and thought it was just a gag. At any rate, they said if a wild man suddenly rushed on the field and tackled one of the players, they'd go get him. We could be sure of it.

The third quarter arrived and our quivering mechanic had managed to consume half of his quart of courage. U.C.L.A. was leading by a small margin. The crowd stirred anxiously. St. Mary's Pre-Flight had the play. Frankie Albert, the great All-American halfback, took the ball on an end-around and galloped goalward. He was hit by a hefty U.C.L.A. lineman and brought to earth. Shaking the dust from his powerful frame, Frankie walked slowly back to his side of the line.

At this point something whirred in our mechanic's brain. His feet began to churn the earth. His coattails flew behind him. And he went for Frankie Albert like a bee for its honey.

Wham! The mechanic hit Albert like a ton of lead . . . and bounced off like a rubber ball! The surprised Albert turned around. A hurt look flashed across his face.

The mechanic rose to his feet and went for Frankie again. He caught an arm and began to pull. The husky Albert, still stunned by the surprise, whirled around. The mechanic held on. Round and round they went, the mechanic flying through the air like a ballet dancer. It looked like a cat trying to shake flypaper off its feet.

Eventually our man let go and sprawled out on the turf. Frankie towered over him and gently suggested, "Look, Bud, why don't you go back to your seat and behave like a nice fella?"

John and I were beside ourselves. The two dumb cops who had agreed to chase our man on the field and grab him before he did—or came to—any real harm stood rooted in sheer astonishment. But two more alert officers—from the *other* side of the field—were on the job. They rushed out, grabbed our mechanic, and dragged him up the steps of the great Coliseum, through the yelling U.C.L.A. cheering section, and out of sight between two massive iron gates. I began breathing again. The stands quieted down.

The game was resumed. There was no sign of our late-lamented contestant. John and I were beginning to worry. Had they taken him off to jail? Would we be sued? Was it our fault if the two cops had upset the applecart with their stupidity?

The game was over. The fans stood up and started lazily milling toward the gates and home. The Guedels and the Linkletters remained in their box. As the last of the crowd slowly passed through the tunnels and the batteries of flood-lights began to fade, a small voice at my elbow spoke up. It was our contestant, none the worse for wear but completely sober. He wanted his hundred-dollar bill.

"Those cops gave me a working-over," he explained. "But when I finally made it clear that I was a 'People Are Funny' contestant, they turned me loose and told me to go on home and quit drinking. The only thing was they turned me loose *outside* the Coliseum . . . and I couldn't get in before this, because I didn't have a ticket!"

I gave him his hundred dollars and congratulated him. After all, none of us was in jail!

It was during the war, those harum-scarum early days when the Allies were getting the worst of it on all fronts and the papers were filled with scare stories of spies and sabo-teurs and dangling parachutists.

Folks in Red Bank, New Jersey, reported they thought they "saw a parachute open high above Farmer Jones' corn-field." (They never saw him land.) Somebody in Ham-on-Rye, England, thought he "saw a parachutist over Tuffington Bogs." (He never saw him land.) A trapper in the Columbia Basin in our own Northwest figured as how he "seen a big white thing through the trees up in the sky." (But he "never seen 'm land.")

So we decided we'd have some fun about it. Since people were parachute-crazy, we'd go parachute-crazy too. It wasn't too difficult . . . for us.

Using the same tried-and-true technique we used with the volunteer who tackled Frankie Albert in the football thriller, we tricked a willing contestant into offering to do just about anything we asked him. Like most of our guests, he said yes to everything.

"With all of these parachute scares and people in a mood to pitchfork anything even resembling a parachutist, what do you suppose would happen, Mr. So-and-so, if one of the contestants on our show suddenly dropped out of the sky into some part of Los Angeles?"

He gulped.

"Would you be willing to help us find out . . . for, say . . . fifty bucks?"

He gulped again and nervously said, "Sure!"

With that he was committed. Assistants hurriedly brought out a parachute, regulation size, and strapped it on him. We gravely instructed him to return it if it didn't open, so we would get our money back. We gave him a flyer's helmet, a book of instructions, and our best wishes. He was game all the way through.

The joke had gone far enough at this point. After all, he had agreed to go through with it, and . . . well, that was all we were after. But we had a basically sound experiment on our hands and we wanted to test it. So we told our shivering parachutist that he really wouldn't have to jump. Instead we had George Waltz, a famous jumper, all set to leap at Metropolitan airport. He, Waltz, was going to do the jumping for our contestant. What we really were after, we explained, was to find out just what people would do if a man in a parachute dropped out of the sky and into the limits of the city of Los Angeles.

Strapped to the back of the professional jumper was an NBC pack transmitter. As I explained the stunt, Waltz's plane took off from the airport, climbed rapidly, and in a few seconds was circling over the city. In the plane was a receiver, tuned to "People Are Funny."

"Now in a few seconds George Waltz is going to jump from the plane over the city. Through the portable pack transmitter on his back he'll be able to describe for us just what reactions he gets from suspicious people on the ground," I explained. "Okay, George Waltz, let 'er go!" And we switched to the jumper.

There were a few seconds of silence as Waltz left the plane. Then he began to talk:

"I'm now free of the ship, and falling fast. Now I've pulled the rip cord, releasing the silk umbrella . . . There it goes . . . Uhhhh." Here a few grunts as he caught the shock of the opening parachute. "Now my descent has been arrested and I'm slowly swinging to earth. I'm over Beverly Hills, where the traffic isn't too congested, and I'm going to head toward a big vacant space down there on the ground. . . . I can see a few people pointing up at me . . . but I don't see any pitchforks in their hands. . . . So far it is a very peace— Hey! What was that?" A slight pause. "Hey! There it is again! . . . Hey! . . . Somebody's shooting at me! . . . There are four holes in this parachute now. . . . Migawd!"

My heart sank. What an experiment! We'd figured spy-conscious residents would get worked up over the parachute, but we never figured they'd shoot at it! A thousand bloody thoughts whirled through my head, all of them having to do with headlines screaming that Art Linkletter had practically murdered a professional parachute jumper!

As Waltz gave his report of the shooting, those of us in the studio stood paralyzed. There was nothing we could do. Then the signal from the pack transmitter went dead. For all we knew, Waltz was a goner. After he'd reported four holes in his chute, there was an awful silence. We looked at each other, at our quaking contestant in his contraption on the stage, and at the shreds of our script.

John was the first one of us to come to. Frantically he pointed to our contestant. Frantically he made motions signaling me to continue on with the show.

I did some split-second thinking. Well, I concluded, it isn't going to do any good to worry out loud over a coast-to-coast network. We might as well pretend Waltz made it okay and it was all part of the show. So I again turned to the contestant.

"Well, that gives you an idea the fun we have on our show," I chattered. "Now for the last part of the stunt. Mr. Blank, we want to find out what people will do if they discover a parachutist hanging in a neighborhood tree. And that's where you come in. We have a specially built derrick, mounted on a truck outside. That truck is going to rush you over to a nearby residential section, sneak up an alley, and hang you up in a tree by your parachute. As soon as you're ready, you start screaming, to get the attention of people in the house. Then, after you've been there long enough to cause some excitement, unhook yourself, get down from the tree, and rush back here to tell us what happened."

The man nodded and we rushed him out into the dusk of early evening.

Still dazed at the thought of Waltz's probable demise, I went ahead with the other stunts on the show.

As we went into the final stages of that memorable night, our contestant returned. He had quite a story. As soon as he'd been properly dangled from the tree by his opened chute, he started to scream. Neighbors came running from houses in the entire block, climbed fences, broke gates, and trampled flowers and shrubs.

"Some thought I was a sure-enough Nazi," he grinned. "Others thought I was a Russian. Most of 'em thought I was an American who had bailed out of an ailing plane. They got me down pretty fast and started shooting questions at me. I explained who I was and came back here."

At this point Guedel came over with a smile a mile wide. Breaking a long-standing, unwritten rule on the show, he interrupted my interview with the contestant:

"Gee, Link," he said, "I just got a call from Waltz. He's

all right. He landed in a vacant lot in Beverly Hills. Those were bullet holes in his parachute, all right. He doesn't know who was shooting at him, but from the size of the holes he figures it was a small-caliber rifle and that it must have been a couple of kids out hunting rabbits in the hills."

The sigh of relief I emitted from coast to coast must have sounded like a punctured tire.

"And you know what?" continued John, and his smile was even broader. "Guess who was the first person to drive up and offer to give him help? None other than Don Thornburgh, vice-president of the Columbia Broadcasting System! Thornburgh took one look at the NBC pack transmitter, snarled 'People Are Funny,' and drove off in a huff!"

America is a nation of sporting, chance-taking gamblers, whether the thrill of winning involves an innocent church raffle where the prize is a home-knitted afghan or a long-shot selling plater at Hialeah. Some of our most popular quiz shows are based completely on the element of taking a chance for a rich prize.

The networks are very strict in their interpretations of what is and what is not a "lottery." Almost every month we run up against the censors in the effort to capitalize on this important element of modern civilization, and the ways to get around the objections are sometimes almost unbelievable.

Actually a true "lottery" depends upon three legs: a prize, a chance, and a consideration. Most of the arguments revolve around "consideration," since program producers insist that no one has to pay anything or buy anything in order to win the prizes offered. However, equally objectionable is the "chance" element, and on this point the networks differ radically.

We wanted to give away a large sum of money on the "House Party" to any studio guest who happened to have in her purse a certain item. Since one of my familiar gimmicks is to go looking through women's purses, the stunt is identified with me and we could see no reason why we wouldn't be allowed to conduct a contest. But the network said "No." It would, they added, be a lottery, since the person winning would do so through sheer luck.

Guedel and I burned gallons of midnight oil figuring out an answer. It was easy, once we saw it: We devised a riddle, hiding clues to the identity of the item in the lines. That made the contest one of skill, since listeners planning on attending the show could solve the riddle, bring the hunted item with them, and win the prize. The network saw it our way and we started the contest.

This is the riddle: "I'm as crooked as a dog's hind leg, and in my time I've brought millions to their lowest level." We offered a hundred dollars the first day to the woman who had that item in her handbag, and each day we added another hundred. We found buttonhooks, corkscrews, loaded dice (a nice try, eh?), a racing form, a Nazi swastika, a pair of men's socks, and numerous other items.

With the prize mounting each time I mentioned the riddle, it wasn't long before telegrams, phone calls, and letters came pouring in from every hamlet in America. Utter strangers stopped me on the street, in restaurants, in theaters, and in my office building, slyly offering me half of my own money if I'd give them a chance to win the cash. One woman drove three hundred and fifty miles to Hollywood, borrowing the family car and telling her husband she was going to a P.T.A. convention, in order to appear on the show.

When the prize reached nine hundred dollars, a woman showed up with the correct answer to the riddle in her purse. Have you guessed it? Yep! A banana!

The riddle was so successful on "House Party" we tried it again on "People Are Funny" a few weeks later, starting the prize money at five hundred dollars. We asked each contestant: "My house has no windows, no roof, no floors; all it has is just two doors. What am I?"

As soon as this one started, all the interest shown in the banana question was quadrupled. People wired they would fly out from Boston if I'd guarantee them a chance to answer. They wanted to come from Florida and Oregon and Minnesota and New Orleans. They wrote and telephoned and wired. Of course we insisted only contestants on the program were eligible. Mail came in at the rate of five hundred letters a day, with each delivery bringing more and more.

We added one hundred dollars to the prize money each week and finally reached twelve hundred dollars. It was quite a plum. Tickets to "People Are Funny" were at a premium. Scalpers who obtained a few through bribery and skulduggery were selling them at five dollars each, then ten dollars.

The answer? A young couple from Texas "thought" it was an oyster. I handed them twelve hundred dollars in cash!

Everybody has a streak of the gambler in him. No matter how strait-laced a person may be, that streak is present someplace. For life itself is a gamble and we're all used to it.

We haven't overlooked this human frailty in our analyses of people and frequently employ the principles of gambling in our tests on the show.

Our excursions into the gambling spirit have usually taken the form of chance-taking decisions. Our "Pick-a-Box" stunt is an ideal example. In this short but hair-raising experiment the contestant is told that we are attempting to discover the accuracy of "intuition" or "hunch." He is confronted by a table on which half a dozen different boxes have been placed. They are all identical in size and shape, and on top of each there are letters describing the possible contents. On one, for instance, the word might be "Cash," or "Pie," or "Ring," or "Tomato," or "Cream Puff." The guest is then told that in some regrettable way the contents of the boxes have become mixed so that no one knows exactly what is in each box, and that if he cares to, he can make a selection of the boxes, providing he agrees to take immediately whatever is inside the box he chooses. We have never had a refusal from anyone, and on the first trial, when there were six boxes, in which were two good prizes and four penalties, the young fellow unerringly selected the box which said "Chocolate Meringue Pie" and, in spite of all of my warnings, he stuck by his decision and took home with him a five-hundred-dollar diamond ring! The next two guests on subsequent programs were not quite so sure . . . or quite so lucky.

An even more amusing version of this gamble was the device where we gave a contestant the opportunity of having either of two buckets upturned on his head. One of the buckets was specially constructed of transparent Plexiglas and from beneath you could see right through it and determine that it was almost full of a clear liquid. The other bucket was an ordinary galvanized iron affair whose contents, of course, could not be seen. I told him that if he selected the plastic bucket, he would get a twenty-dollar bill no matter what happened when the contents were upturned over his head. However, if he selected the solid bucket and agreed to receive on himself whatever was held therein, he might get something better, or worse: who could tell?

There was an interesting psychological question. Would he take the sure-thing prize of twenty dollars and a simple wetting, or would he gamble on a bigger prize and consequently the chance of a bigger penalty?

The studio audience was yelling its advice to "Take the tin bucket!" But I cautioned him that HE was the one who would have to pay the price of a wrong decision. At first he indicated that he would take the mystery bucket. And then I pointed out that it might very well be filled with oatmeal or spaghetti or hot tar. He thought this over, wavered in his decision, and finally thought perhaps the sure twenty bucks would be best. While the crowd shrieked its objections, I brought up the interesting conjecture that the liquid might NOT be water, but rather *could* be maple syrup, and further that the mystery bucket might have in it an order for a new car or a suit of clothes or a trip to Mexico City.

By this time the poor fellow was in a terrible state, and my carefully thought out plan of cross-examination wasn't helping him any. Members of the audience almost had to be forcibly restrained from leaping onto the stage to take a more convincing part in the argument.

When I judged the suspense had reached its peak, I quieted everyone and announced that he had one last chance to make up his mind by himself with no suggestions from anyone. The befuddled guest looked suspiciously at both buckets and then picked the metal one, just as we had guessed he would all along. My assistant pulled the cord, the bucket turned over, and down came a flood of water . . . drenching him thoroughly. Then, while we were drying him off and waiting for the laughs to subside, I directed that the plastic bucket be turned over to see what would have happened if he had selected that one. The cord was pulled, the pail flipped over, and NOTHING spilled out, because the top had been sealed over with a plastic sheet! Then, while groans of disappointment and chagrin rose from the crowd, announcer Rod O'Connor came up and said, "Art, here's something I found on the floor that must have spilled out of that first bucket along with the water."

How surprised I was to discover that it was a small cylinder inside of which, by some strange chance, there nestled a hundred-dollar bill!

Still another form of gambling which was utilized in one of our stunts occurred at the height of the meat shortage. A young couple was selected and quizzed about whether or not they would purchase and eat government-inspected horse meat if they could not get a supply of regular meat for their home consumption. The wife said she didn't think so, while the husband thought it wouldn't be so bad; especially since he had spent two years in a Jap prison camp and had become accustomed to eating anything that came his way. I told them that we were interested in conducting a poll to discover what the average citizen would say to the same question and gave each of them a telephone book, a handful of nickels, and a telephone booth to use in calling numbers at random for the next few minutes.

While they were busy with this, I unveiled our Machiavellian plot to the audience. We had two big, juicy hamburger sandwiches brought on stage, and I explained that when the husband and wife returned we would pay them one hundred dollars if they would both take bites out of both sandwiches. However, I pointed out, I was going to tell them that ONE of those sandwiches had horse meat in it and the other was standard steer meat. As usual, I then spent about twenty seconds pleading with the studio listeners NOT to tip off our guests.

When they returned with their report of the telephone calls (half and half, out of some fifteen contacts), I gave each of them a sandwich and explained the proposition. At first both the husband and wife refused to take a bite out of either bun. Then the husband broke down and said that he would go for the deal if she would. But the wife remained obstinate. I waved the hundred-dollar bill in front of them and asked him if he'd give her the whole amount if she'd break down and take the bites. He thought for a moment and then agreed to the gamble. Then, with both of us working on her, she at last agreed and they went to work on the sandwiches.

I have never seen such puffed-up cheeks on any living creature but a squirrel in autumn. The wife *took* the bites but she just couldn't *swallow* them. To my questions she mumbled that the first sandwich was the horse meat and it just wouldn't go down. While the audience howled their delight, the ex-soldier husband ventured the opinion that neither of them was horse meat. When I broke down and agreed, an expression of vast relief crossed his wife's face and down went the bites in four big swallows. Then followed an unexpected bit of comedy-drama, for when I handed the missus the hundred dollars, friend husband got hold of a corner of it and a good-natured tug of war occurred while the married folks in the audience cheered for one side or the other.

Husbands always seem to be ready to stand up for another of their kind in any staged controversy, and wives can be expected to be equally stanch in their defense of other wives. So we made this the basis for an unusual experiment that involved both gambling and domestic psychology during the Christmas season.

Selecting a couple from the audience, we told the husband that we wanted to see if he could prevent his wife from locating him within an area of three city blocks before the end of the program if we gave him a two-minute start. And then after he was gone, we told his wife that it was just a ruse to get him away and let him play cops and robbers with himself for the rest of the show while actually she would be buying him a Christmas present as a surprise. We gave her a hundred-dollar bill and told her to pick out anything she wanted for him and she could keep the change for herself. THEN, after she had gone out to make the purchase, we brought the husband back in and told him that we had kept him in a dressing room only long enough to send the wife on a wild-goose chase after him but that actually he would be out buying a Christmas present for the wife. We gave him a hundred-dollar bill and told him that anything left over from his wife's present would be his own spending money.

The question was: Which one would spend the most money on a present for the other, thus having less money for himself out of the hundred dollars?

With a roving microphone I next went down into the studio audience for opinions and bets on the above question, and sure enough, the men were anxious to bet on the man's generosity and the women were ready to vouch for the lady's big heart. I distributed red and green cards, depending on the choice.

Before NBC would permit any of this speculation to occur, I had to agree that in my opening interviews with the couple, before the actual stunt got under way, I would question them generally about Christmas and what they had given each other the preceding Christmas. This, you see, gave the audience some factual information about the couple, and therefore the element of "skill" would enter into their betting and scandalous "chance" would be eliminated.

At any rate, the end of the show brought back our couple with their "surprise" gifts for each other . . . and what do you think happened?

The wife had spent fifty-five dollars on her husband's gift. The husband had spent sixty-three on his wife's gift.

Both bought watches.

To each of our winners in the audience went a special gift of a portable radio.

"Backfires" from our outside stunts provide amusing and complex situations to be disentangled hours or even days after the actual broadcast. I'll never forget the night we had a woman contestant drop "SOS" notes from a Hollywood hotel window on which were scribbled in lipstick: "Am being held by ruffians in Room 617. HELP!" She was promptly "rescued" by a passing sailor on whom one of the messages fell, and they returned to the studio where he was appropriately rewarded and quizzed.

But, unbeknown to us, several of the frantic appeals had been blown to one of the ledges of the hotel building and stayed there until another breeze released them to the street below a few nights later. Room 617 by then was occupied by a paying guest who was completely oblivious of the trick which fate had prepared for her.

"Open the door or we'll break it down!" came the gruff orders of the squad of policemen outside Room 617. And while the poor gal shook in her nightgown, the would-be rescuers ransacked the place for the fiendish "kidnapers."

That one took some tall fixing.

Then there was the incident of the "Real Plumber."

Bill West is a plumber employed by the AA-1 Plumbing Company of Hollywood. Bill has made numerous professional calls at the home of Jack Stanley, one of the writers of "People Are Funny."

From this meager fact came a hilarious stunt. We called it the "Real Plumber." Here's the way it worked.

Bill waited until we had an opportune moment on the show. The day before we were scheduled to use the "Real Plumber" stunt, Bill answered an emergency call at the home of a couple living in the neighborhood of NBC's pale green studios. The woman of the house said she had a leaky faucet in her kitchen. Would Bill come over and fix it? Bill certainly would.

He answered the call the next morning. It was a Friday morning. He entered the house, shut off all the water, removed the faucet, removed the pipe, went into the bathroom, removed several faucets there, and went back to his shop.

An hour or so later he returned to the house, took out the sink, disconnected the sanitary tub in the porch, knocked on the wall between porch and kitchen, and said the wall would have to come out. Then he went back to his shop.

This went on all day. He strewed plumbers' tools all over the house, banged on pipes, suggested ominous things to the horrified mistress of the house, and went back and forth between shop and customer. He could see her temperature rising noticeably.

He made his last call at five o'clock in the evening, and as he again returned to his shop he removed a tube from the householder's radio, thereby silencing it for what was to come.

At six o'clock (Pacific Time) "People Are Funny" took to

the air. One of the first guests to be introduced was Bill West, plumber for the AA-1 Plumbing Company, of Hollywood.

Bill described his work, then settled down to an account of his latest job. In minute detail he admitted the monstrous things he had been doing all day long.

"I'll bet the woman of that house is pretty sore at you by now," I prompted.

"She's pretty mad all right," replied Bill. "You see, I'm getting a dollar and a half an hour for the job. It really should have cost her about seventy-five cents, but at the present time her bill is somewhere in the neighborhood of forty-five dollars!"

"But gee, Bill," I went on as if I didn't know, "if it is an emergency, what are you doing here? Why aren't you over there fixing the leaky faucet?"

"Oh, I wanted to go to the basketball game tonight," said the errant plumber. "I'm sending my assistant over to finish the job tonight."

"And who is your assistant?"

"I don't know yet."

All eyes turned toward a gulping contestant who was waiting in line for the evening's fun. The situation needed no tip-off from me. It introduced itself glibly.

"Well, well . . . Mister Jones! Do . . . you . . . know . . . where . . . we . . . can . . . find . . . an . . . assistant?"

Feebly he murmured, "Noo—oo."

Confidently I reassured him. "Well, I know where we can find one. Hel-lo, Mis-ter Jones!"

Quickly, before the drama of the situation could fade, we put the shuddering contestant in a pair of coveralls, on the back of which was embroidered "AA-1 Plumbing." Quickly we instructed him to get over to the suffering householder and repair the leak. He left like a rocket.

The contestant returned at the end of the program. With him was an elderly couple, obviously bewildered by the wicked twist of fortune that had befallen them that horrible day.

Bit by bit the story came out. The mistress of the house told of the real plumber's fumbling efforts, of her inconvenience, of her anger at the turn of events, of her having to go next door to take a bath. She described her despair when our phony assistant plumber made even worse efforts to repair the damage.

When the full story had been told, we apologized to our innocent victims, assigned Bill West, the real plumber, to set to work immediately to repair the damage, gave the victims a big dinner and a night at Earl Carroll's, and to top it off gave them a beautiful General Electric refrigerator. Everybody was happy and all was forgiven.

As the elderly couple bowed in acknowledgment of the applause from the studio audience, I had a passing thought. "What," I asked the husband, "do you do for a living?"

The old man smiled sadly as he answered. And his answer brought down the house. "I work," he said slowly, "for the Los Angeles Bureau of Water and Power!"

The "House Party": The Kids

PITY THE PRESIDENT OF THE UNITED STATES! THE YOUTH of today doesn't want his job!

The small fry will be happy cowboys, policemen, plumbers, carpenters, doctors, dentists, and even garbage men. But President? Not on your life!

For more than fourteen years now I've been asking boys what they'd like to be when they grow up. That question is the outstanding feature of the daily "House Party." The majority want to be policemen, "because policemen carry guns." Second choice is for a life on the open range, and the fact that cowboys carry guns (at least the motion-picture variety) has not a little to do with the decision. I make a point every day to ask at least one of my junior guests if he'd like to be President someday. And without exception the answer is "No!"

Reasons for the declination are widely assorted: one tyke said he was "satisfied with George Washington." Another said the President "travels around too much" and he'd rather stay home. A number have agreed that the President's job is "too tough" and "people are always blaming him for things."

After putting the question to over five thousand boys between the ages of five and thirteen, I've reached the conclusion that when the younger generation matures, the United States is going to be hard put to find a Chief Executive!

To an amateur psychologist and philosopher like myself, the results of my one-man poll are fascinating. The youngsters, after all, pretty accurately reflect the opinions and ideas of their parents. And if the children scorn the presidency . . . well, I'd say it is an unpopular job, by unanimous consent!

The school boys and girls are influenced in their thinking by what they hear at home, on the radio, and by what they see in the movies. It is no surprise, therefore, that most little girls would like to be movie stars. Second choice is that of housewife, and nursing comes third.

But no matter how much they may be influenced, I've discovered most normal children have definite ideas and plans and dreams of their own. And their reasoning is solid and well considered. For instance, a little Chinese boy once told me how he wanted to be a dentist, "because doctors have to get up in the middle of the night and deliver babies!" That makes sense, doesn't it?

A little girl soberly admitted she'd like to be a housewife and a mother. When I asked her why, she explained, "Because then my mummy could be a grandmummy!"

Children are small grownups, and, all things being relative, their perspectives are therefore the same as adults, only diminished. Children are serious and given, in their own ways, to serious thinking. A small boy will give as much deliberation and careful consideration to a dollar bill as his father will to one hundred dollars. I once asked an eight-year-old if he planned to marry when he grew up. He was terribly serious when he answered, "No, I don't think so. The marriage license costs too much!" (His daddy thinks the down payment is reasonable enough, but the upkeep is expensive.)

The parents of a thirteen-year-old junior-high-school girl learned a great deal about their daughter during her appearance as my guest on the "House Party." I only hope they took the hint and helped her out. She had told me, on the air, that she'd like to be "ten years old for the rest of my life!"

In amazement I wondered why.

"Well," she explained with a touch of sadness, "then I wouldn't have to know about the facts of life!"

Of all the programs I've done in my nineteen years on the air, I think I personally enjoy doing the daily "House Party" broadcast best of all. People are natural, friendly, and talkative, and therefore interesting and fun. And the "House Party's" easygoing construction permits me the pleasure of dealing with the best types of all to interview: kids and old folks. The latter have nothing to hide; they don't care what others think, so tell all. The kids, on the other hand, don't know what they don't know, so they tell all too!

The boys and girls who visit us every day are plain, normal, average youngsters who are selected not because they're unusually bright or trained or talented but because they're just kids. I don't want "Quiz Kids"; I prefer just kids, for they're much more amusing and entertaining.

Where else but from the "kid next door" would you get comedy like that provided by one youngster who defined a "politician" as being a "man in the government who solves problems that wouldn't be there if there weren't politicians in the first place!" Or the junior physician who had a sure cure for the hiccups. "When people have the hiccups, I just hit 'em over the head," he explained with all the seriousness of an intern. The little boy who wanted to be a garbage man someday had made his choice because "garbage men bang the cans down on the sidewalk in the morning and wake people up!" Another wanted to join a circus and be a "lion container"! (He said he thought he could "contain" about five lions!)

Parents often ask me why their children behave so well when I talk to them in front of a microphone with four or five hundred people in the audience. The usual complaint is: "Junior becomes shy or smart-alecky when *I* try to show him off at home!"

The answer is simple: Parents too often treat their children as children. I don't. I treat them as small adults! I don't poke fun at them, ridicule their ideas, nor scoff at their opinions. As a result the children, in turn, treat me as an equal. We get along fine.

I've often wondered about the parents of one scientifically minded ten-year-old boy who visited me on the "House Party." The lad had admitted his ambition to be an astronomer. Suddenly, as if relieving himself of a problem that had bothered him for weeks, he asked me: "Why is it that it is colder in the mountains, where it is closer to the sun, than it is in the valleys, which are farther away from the sun?"

Sure it was an odd question. And I confess I didn't have a ready answer. But if that boy had asked his parents the same question, what would their answer have been? It was an important question to the boy, but it was an even more important question for the parents. If they sloughed him off with a silly answer, he would in the future think twice before asking them a serious question. If they bothered to look up a sincere answer, the boy would have been encouraged to explore still deeper into mysteries of his world. That little man was in an important phase of his life; his parents held the key to his future.

I don't have to wonder about the future of another little boy who appeared as my guest. This youngster was an average boy of nine years, a little shy, modest, and somewhat uncomfortable after sitting in a hard chair for fifteen minutes. He was not a particularly bright boy to begin with. It was understandable, then, that he didn't know his last name when I began talking with him for the benefit of the listening audience. And he didn't know his father's name, the name of his school, nor his father's business. He just didn't know anything because he was frightened. I passed by him quickly; after all, there was no sense in emphasizing his reticence.

After the show I strolled out in the artists' corridor behind the studio in Hollywood. There was the little boy, undergoing a session with his angry mother. "You do *too* know your last name!" she stormed, and gave him a shake. "You do *too* know your father's name!" Another shake, "You do *too* know where your father works!" A rattling good shake. I hurried out to my car and rushed home to my own kids.

There have been five little Links on the Linkletter chain: Jack, Dawn, Robert, Sharon and Diane. They're like any other children, with one exception: When young Jack concluded his prayers at night, he proved he was a member of a radio family by adding: "Listen in again tomorrow night, same time, same station, for another in this series!"

I caught him standing on the curb outside our Hollywood home one afternoon, stopping passers-by. As I stood behind a neighboring tree, I heard him say to an elderly gentleman: "Good afternoon. I'm Jack Linkletter. Would you mind saying a few words to our listeners? First of all, your name, sir?"

The elderly gentleman hurried on his way as fast as he could walk.

Young Jack wanted to be an ad-libber too. And I encouraged him by conducting little interview sessions at every opportunity. Once we took a week-end auto trip to the mountains. All the way to our destination Link and I interviewed each other. I'd pretend I was a famous aviator, then he'd assume the role of the master of ceremonies and ask me questions. I purposely gave answers that were designed to make him think. For instance, I'd say I'd jumped out of my plane and my parachute failed to open . . . to see how he'd frame his next question.

He proved his nimble wit by switching to another interview in the rear seat: Mrs. Linkletter!

From my home sessions with the little Linkletters I discover the tricks that will work when I'm on the air with my young guests at the "House Party." It helps considerably in pursuing an interview that threatens to become simply a series of monosyllabic grunts.

A case in point is that of a serious little fellow I found in front of me one afternoon at the show. He was about seven, wore thick horn-rimmed glasses, and to all intents and purposes was a mature little boy. After a brief answer or two he finally told me his father was a professor of child psychology at Los Angeles City College. That tipped me off that here was an unusual youngster. "What else does your daddy do?" I asked.

"Oh, he coaches a little too," was the reply.

"And whom does he coach?" I inquired further.

He frowned disgustedly and muttered: "The dopes on the football team!"

Often I ask my young guests questions designed to test their powers of logic. Take the time the little boy defined "forefathers" as "a father with four heads." And then there's the time a little girl, with sound reasoning, concluded that inasmuch as a "widow" was a "lady without a husband," a "grass widow" would naturally become a "grasshopper without a husband"!

I asked a sixth-grader whom she'd rather marry, a city fellow or a country fellow, and the answer was in favor of the former, "as he'd be more civilized"!

One of the best laugh-getters was the time the seven-year-old reported she had once milked a cow, "but," she added, "I never did get much out of it!"

In New York a city boy was asked how to go about getting the milk from a cow. He recommended cutting it open, draining the milk, and making Italian meat balls with the remainder of the carcass!

The Los Angeles Board of Education has been extremely co-operative in helping us obtain the school kids every day. But before we could set up the routine as a permanent part of our show, we first had to guarantee that the children would not be exploited, ridiculed, or shown at any disadvantage either to themselves or to their parents. As a result of this wise precaution, we engaged the services of a certified teacher of the California school system.

Each day she appears at a previously selected school in a special chauffeured limousine. The five youngsters are taken from their classrooms, brought to the studios, taken on a tour of the building, given a lunch of their own choosing in a famous Hollywood restaurant, and then introduced to me a half hour before the show.

I have a fifteen-minute session before we go on the air, during which I become acquainted with them. I laugh and kid and learn as much as I can about them. By air time we're all good friends and ready for some fun on stage. I don't coach them in advance nor do I suggest things for them to say. As a matter of fact, they often tell me one thing in our pre-broadcast session and exactly the opposite during the show.

I'll never forget one little boy who, in the pre-broadcast chat, advised me his father was a special investigator for the

FBI. "He carries a gun and chases crooks and spies and things," he confessed. When we got together before my microphone, I started to lead into this exciting description.

"Tell me, Buster, what does your daddy do?"

"He's a streetcar conductor," was the astonishing answer, and nothing I could do would make him change it.

For sheer comedy and human interest, kids are the finest natural entertainers in show business. What gag writer in radio could possibly think of original material like the following?

I asked a nine-year-old girl what her mother did. "She's a typewriter," was the reply. I asked a young bobby-soxer what three items she'd take along if she were to be cast a-shore on a desert island. In all seriousness she answered: "I'd take along three bobby pins, as my hair is not naturally curly and I would like to look as nice as possible when I was rescued!"

A seven-year-old boy admitted he wanted to be a "scientist who studies outside the world." A six-year-old girl described her boy friend as follows: "Well . . . he's got blue eyes . . . and . . . uh . . . blond hair . . . and . . . uh . . . *brown pants!*"

"You've got some teeth missing!" I said to a six-year-old tyke. "How'd it happen they're coming out so early?"

"Oh," was his explanation, "I ran into a door!"

And a classic is the little fellow who announced he had a baby brother with whom he played when Mother was busy with the housekeeping. I asked him how he went about playing with a tiny baby brother, and his answer stopped me for a moment. "I play with a pillow and a gun," he confessed. "It's easy. I just put the pillow over him to keep him quiet, then *I* play with the gun!"

I noticed that one of my young male guests had particularly wavy hair and said so, asking how it got that way.

"Oh, I had a permanent wave two days ago because my hair kept falling down all over my face!" was the answer.

A little girl said she'd like to be "a singer, or a musician, or an artist, or a writer" when she grew up, but sadly added she'd probably "just be a housewife . . . because it's been handed down through the family."

A seven-year-old told me his father was a hot-dog maker, so I asked: "What does your mother do?"

"Oh, nothing," he shrugged. "She's too busy having babies!"

I asked a bright little boy what he was giving up during the Lenten season. He thought a moment and gave me the truth: "Everything except food and candy!"

"I know my big white kitty is listening in at home because I told him to and he said, 'Yes, I will!' " was the amazing statement of a little elf with large brown eyes. She's going to have a wonderful time in this old world!

Imagine the consternation of a proud father when he heard his offspring say: "No, I don't think I want to grow up to be just like my daddy!" When I asked him why, he merely assumed an arched-eyebrow attitude and replied: "Oh, I have my reasons!"

A little girl told me she was "one half Polish, one half Italian, and one half American"! Another confessed she had some unusual pets—three Mexican jumping beans! A music student revealed his two favorite classical compositions were "Silent Night, Holy Night" and "Birmingham Jail"! A teen-ager described a high-school pajama party as being the time "when a bunch of us old maids get together in our pajamas in somebody's house with some food and wish the boys would come over!"

A number of boys want to be cowboys, although most of them have never been on a horse. I once asked a tyke to tell me what a horse looks like. "Well . . . it . . . uh . . . has two legs in front . . . and . . . uh . . . (triumphantly) TWO LEGS IN BACK!"

A six-year-old girl admitted she had some dolls—three little bears. She calls them "Goodnik, Foofnik, and Pugnik!" A chubby little boy surprised me by his reading habits. It seemed he thoroughly enjoyed *The Bobbsey Twins, Neighbors and Helpers,* and the Encyclopaedia Britannica! I asked him to spell the latter and he did so without hesitation. Realizing I had something unusual, I pried further: "What did you find in the Encyclopaedia?"

With a trace of boredom he sighed: "Not much!"

Any peg upon which to hang a question that might bring out a strange answer is never overlooked. A little girl told me she'd recently had an operation and further pointed out she'd had her appendix removed. "I put it in a glass jar and showed it to all my friends at school," she explained.

A young man of nine years was right when he said: "The President of the United States is Mr. Roosevelt." He was a trifle confused, however, when he said: "The President before President Roosevelt was Abraham Lincoln!"

Little George was asked if he had any girl friends. He blushed a little and nudged a nine-year-old charmer sitting next to him on the stage. A moment later I asked him what three things he'd choose to take with him if he were to become stranded on a desert island. He blushed again, and again nudged the little charmer sitting next to him!

I hope his mother wasn't too hard on little Benny when he told me he was going to celebrate Halloween by "throwing baseballs at my mamma's dishes"!

And I'll bet a lot of parents blushed when I asked my five young guests: "Should parents help their children with homework?" All five said "No"! (It seems like parents always get the wrong answers!)

A seven-year-old miss admitted her ambition in life was to be "a common housewife." And a five-year-old defined "alimony" as simply "marriage"! A little boy said his greatest ambition in life was to be a dry cleaner!

I asked another little boy if he knew how to shoot pool. "No," he murmured, "I don't even know how to swim!"

Little Phillip Wood owns a goat. He feeds it "alfa-alfa." I

wanted to know if he also fed his pet tin cans. "No," he stated, "because it would make the milk taste!"

When I asked Billy Taylor what his father did, I received this one: "He's a captain of eye, ear, nose, and throat in the Army!"

The popular consensus among teen-agers as to the proper time to go to bed at night is "midnight"!

One of my favorites came from a pretty, wide-eyed little girl of four years. She was agog at the business of broadcasting and quite aware of the mass of amused faces staring up at her from the seats in front. I asked her to tell me the meaning of an "old maid."

She complied with: "A crabby old lady!" The audience roared, and little Marjorie, shocked, burst into tears. I had to promise her cake, candy, hamburgers, and ice cream after the show in order to bring her back to earth!

During the pre-broadcast session one day, the son of a famous Hollywood star told me his mother had instructed him never to say, "Eeny, meeny, miney, mo: Catch a nigger by the toe," around the house.

"That's right," I cautioned, "it isn't a nice thing to say at all."

The lad wasn't quite finished. "Because," he added, "Mom says the maid will quit if she hears me!"

She was a cutie-pie of only four years of age, with curly brown hair and a pretty brown dress. She had been fairly talkative during our get-acquainted session before we went on the air, but when I came to her during the broadcast she froze.

"And your name is . . . ?" I began.

She shook her head silently.

"You don't know your name? Well, how old are you?"

Another shake of the head.

"Got any boy friends?" I prodded.

She shook her head.

I was getting desperate. "Of course you know what your daddy does?"

At this her eyes grew wide, her mouth dropped open, and with oceans of curiosity she asked, "No! What?"

"Do you have any brothers or sisters?" I asked a little six-year-old miss.

"No, I haven't," she replied, "but I'm going to get a little baby brother!"

"Is that so? When?"

"As soon as my mother gets married again," she reported with personal authority.

A small Negro boy, brushed as neat as a pin, admitted his name was Abraham Lincoln Taylor. I couldn't let it go by unnoticed.

"Gee, that's fine. You know, of course, whom you were named for!"

He nodded, "Yes suh . . . my cousin!"

A particulary well-washed and beribboned blonde of five

years indicated her mother's pride and belief that the tyke belonged on the screen. Doubtless Mama figured this was little Blondie's big opportunity. If it was, little Blondie probably got a walloping when she got home. I had noticed her becoming dimples and mentioned them. "Where did you get those pretty dimples?" I prodded.

"Mommy says I got them" (deep thought) "from the iceman!"

My favorite little boy is one who stands a fine chance of being radio's top ad-libber in the year 1980. At least he's glib enough at the age of seven to come up with an answer, even if it isn't the right one. And that's the first commandment for a radio M.C.

On Washington's Birthday I included several questions to the kids on the Father of Our Country. When I came to one little fellow I asked him to tell me the story of George and the cherry tree. He was going along nicely until he came to the part most often quoted.

"And who was it who cut down the cherry tree?" I prompted.

"George Washington."

"And what did George say when his father asked him who did it?"

He stopped a second, to put himself in young Washington's place. Then came the ringing answer:

"Not me! It was some other kid!"

The "House Party":
The Grown-Up Kids

TWO HUNDRED POUNDS OF TALKATIVE WOMAN STOOD BEfore our "House Party" microphone to describe her "most embarrassing moment."

"I wasn't feeling too well," she began, "and so I decided to take a nice warm tub bath. I was all alone in my apartment. After I had finished my bath, I started to climb out of the tub and I couldn't do it. So I screamed. The manager of the apartment house heard me down the air shaft and sent up the janitor. He had to break the door down to get to me.

"The janitor pulled and tugged and, well, as you can see, I'm pretty heavy, and there I sat. Finally he said: 'You move up under the faucets and I'll get in behind you and shove.' So we tried that and finally he got me up on the edge of the bed."

The talkative, middle-aged woman didn't realize her slip of the tongue, but the audience did and hysteria took over for several minutes.

It's amazing what personal, intimate facts people will reveal about themselves before a transcontinental microphone. Women in particular are startlingly talkative. They'll say anything. I don't know whether it's because they don't realize people from coast to coast are actually listening at the other end of that little innocent microphone or whether they do realize it but just don't care. At any rate, the fact that they *will* talk is the basis for the "House Party" show.

Another woman in the same "House Party" contest described *her* most embarrassing moment.

"My husband and I were traveling on a train from Kansas City," she recalled. "It was late at night and the passengers had retired. I got up to go to the rest room. When I came back in the dim Pullman car, I couldn't see very well. But I found my berth and climbed in. My husband was occupying the middle of the berth and I tried to shove him over. He just grunted and rolled to one side. Then I climbed in and started to talk. His answers to my conversation sounded queer so I switched on the light . . . and found myself in bed with a total stranger!"

The grand-prize winner for the week was a gold-plated dilly. We gave her a washing machine.

"I was getting married," she began. "I had a new suit, but I wanted something old, something borrowed, and something blue to go with it. The only thing I could find at the last moment was an old pair of panties. I put them on and rushed off to church.

"As I went down the aisle toward the altar I felt the rubber band break, and in terror I clasped my prayer book to my stomach to keep my panties from falling.

"Everything went along fine until my new husband and I went into the business of the wedding ring. In the excitement of the moment, I extended my left hand and suddenly felt a threatening give beneath my skirt. Fortunately just then we knelt before the altar and I was saved.

"Happily I arose when the priest finished. I raised on tiptoes to kiss my husband for the first time. And down dropped those darned pants around my ankles.

"I was horrified. Titters spread like a prairie fire in the audience. In a daze I stepped out of the baby-blue underclothes, bent over, picked them up and handed them to my new groom, thinking he'd stuff them in his pocket.

"Instead he took one look, blushed, and handed them back to me!

"A moment later we marched up the aisle, arm in arm. The organ played 'Lohengrin,' my friends smiled. I was the only bride in history to take those immortal steps with a new husband on one arm . . . and a pair of blue panties on the other!"

One woman stood before my microphone and told me in all confidence that her son was adopted and that he didn't know it and that she hoped he would never find it out! She didn't seem to realize five million people were listening to her, including, perhaps, her own adopted son!

One of the regular features of the "House Party" is the "How-I-Met-My-Husband" spot, in which wives describe their first meetings with their present spouses.

Tops for me is the instance when a plump lady from Utah told us that she was occupying an apartment in Long Beach, California, in 1933, when the tragic earthquake struck.

"I rushed out of my room," she recalled, "when the building began to shake. I was terrified, so terrified that I forgot to put on my dress. Out in the hallway I ran right into a gentleman who had just left his room, across from mine. He didn't have any clothes on either. And right there, with the building shaking and the plaster falling, I decided he was the man for me. I married him, too!"

Another time a woman related how she was a patient in a hospital when a slight quake shook the building. "I jumped out of bed and ran down the corridor. As I turned a corner I ran smack into a handsome young intern who was carrying a specimen. It spilled all over and we got married three months later!"

"House Party" fans will remember another "first meeting" which we on the show consider one of the best laugh provokers. The fair damsel recalled that it took place at a masquerade ball. "I was dressed as a Spanish señorita," she coyly admitted.

"And how was your husband dressed?" I asked.

"He wasn't dressed at all," smiled the innocent lady. She brought down the house with that one.

A chubby blonde was describing how she first met the lucky man. She told how she did her bit during the war, as a repair worker in a locomotive roundhouse.

"I wore overalls, of course," she smiled prettily. "One day I was stooped over beneath a big engine. Along came this man and I guess he thought I was one of his pals, because he reached over and—"

I started to interrupt at this point because it was pretty obvious what was coming next, but the gal kept right on.

". . . cracked me on the bottom!" she finished. Fortunately it wasn't what I was afraid it was going to be. I'm happy to say she married the gentleman shortly thereafter.

The remarks that bring the biggest laughs are the ones made in complete innocence. The audience loves to watch the flustered look that spreads over a guest's face when she realizes she's slipped. And I never deliberately lead them into it because that would be a dirty trick.

One afternoon our guest of honor was a prominent member of the Hollywood Movie Mothers' Club. She was the mother of two of our best-known screen stars, Olivia de Havilland and Joan Fontaine. I was chatting with her about her famous daughters and the family background. It was wartime.

"Where were the girls born?" I asked casually.

"In Tokyo, Japan," she stated in a matter-of-fact tone.

"In TOKYO!" I exclaimed in surprise. "How in the world did THAT happen?"

"In the regular way!"

There was a moment of silence as the full significance of the answer sank in, then a full minute and a half of appreciative laughter filled CBS from border to border and coast to coast.

Was my face red!

I was playing the "personal-pronoun game" with a young

woman one time. She was fined a quarter every time she said "I" or "me" or "my" or "we," and naturally she was answering my questions as best she could without using one of these personal pronouns. She was doing fine, too, when suddenly I asked her whom her two children resembled. In her anxiety to avoid saying "my husband," she took a flyer and said: "The iceman!" She'll never be the same again!

Another popular "House Party" game requires feminine contestants to criticize their husbands. I give them a dollar for each constructive remark. It usually works out pretty well, except in the case of a middle-aged woman who just couldn't think of a thing wrong with her hubby. I prodded and urged to no avail.

"Aw, come on. Surely you can think of *something* wrong with your husband!"

Silence and deep thought.

I gave up. "Well," I said, "he must be just about perfect!"

My guest sighed profoundly. "He is," she said. "He's a minister!"

Frequently we use women from the studio audience in our commercial messages from the sponsor. It makes entertainment out of otherwise straight selling. The commercials are all written, of course, and there is little chance for anything to go wrong. But people are people, and that means there's margin for error. I'll never forget one woman who had been properly primed in advance by Jack Slattery, our announcer. It was a "gag" commercial and the woman was supposed to know all about electric blankets, one of the products of the sponsor at that time.

"And if it gets cold in the middle of the night, what do you do?" I prompted in all confidence.

"I get up and put my flannels on!" was the show-stopper. I gave her an electric iron for good luck anyway.

Each week at the "House Party" we look for some unusual guest. Sometimes it is the oldest bachelor, or the newest bride, or the woman with the largest feet, or the person farthest from home. As the week progresses, contestants become more numerous and better qualified for the major prize. On Fridays we're pretty sure to have a first-class, A-Number-One winner.

The race was unusually close the time we went looking for the mother with the youngest child. On Monday the winner was two months of age. On Tuesday the baby was only three weeks old. On Wednesday, two weeks. On Thursday, twelve days. And on Friday, when I asked for a show of hands of new mothers in the audience, dozens waved frantically. After questioning them rapidly, the race narrowed until finally only one hand feebly remained in the air.

"And how old is your child?" I wanted to know.

Weakly came the answer: "Six days. This is my first day out of bed!"

I invited the lady to come up on the stage and answer some questions. She came all right . . . accompanied by a registered nurse! I gave her a new refrigerator.

A Santa Fe Railroad conductor, Ernest M. Hazlett, was the winner of our "newest father" contest held a few weeks later. Still shaking, he had been a father only two hours and ten minutes when he showed up on our show. He had been up all night awaiting the event and then had rushed to CBS to win the new G.E. range.

Another participant in the contest admitted his baby hadn't arrived up to air time but that he'd been standing guard at the telephone booth in the lobby of CBS, hoping for a call from the hospital. He too was present on orders from his wife.

Then there was the time we were looking for the mother with the most children. One volunteer admitted she had five and was only thirty-seven years of age.

"Gee!" I exclaimed. "You must spend a lot of time working around the house!"

"Oh no," came the reply. "It isn't work . . . it's just a nice hobby!"

Occasionally, when a guest makes a slip of the tongue, she furiously and unwisely attempts to correct herself. It merely goes from bad to worse, unless I drag her out of it.

An illustration of this human trait developed last fall. A young matron was describing how she met the man she finally married.

"Well," she began confidently, "you see, we were living together in the same house—"

A titter from the audience warned her something was wrong.

"I mean we were living in the same *apartment* house, but in different rooms—"

The titters became snorts.

"I mean . . . well . . . I lived in one room and he lived in another one—"

I felt the time had arrived for me to come to the rescue.

"You lived in the same apartment house but on different floors," I offered, thinking she'd grasp at the straw and follow me to safety. But no . . .

"Well . . . no. It was the same floor, but—"

By this time I was in the quicksand with her. The only thing to do was to start the whole thing over again. We made it the second time.

Just when I decide that *everything* has happened to me and no situation can possibly arise for which I haven't a glib answer, it does!

We were searching for the oldest father of a baby under a year old, and in answer to my query a half dozen elderly candidates raised their hands. Fifty, fifty-four, sixty-three, SIXTY-SEVEN! The winner was sixty-seven years old, his wife was thirty-five, and their infant son had been born just ten days before the broadcast. As the heads of the entire "House Party" audience swiveled around in curiosity to see what this champion looked like, I leaped off the stage and met the winning father halfway down the aisle.

We gabbed about parenthood in general, with me carefully

avoiding the delicate questions everyone was wondering about. And then I finally kidded, "Do you mind if I talk to the youngster?"

"Course not," he wheezed. "Brought him down just in case you wouldn't believe me, and you might as well have a good look. He's on his maw's lap back there next to the last row."

I blissfully charged up the aisle, leaned down over the mother's lap where little Junior reposed beneath a blanket, and inquired, "Is it O.K. to chat with your young man?"

"Sure you can," she replied briskly. "But he's pretty busy right now having his lunch." And with this she threw off the blanket, and there, four inches from the tip of my nose, was Junior nursing away like an animated suction pump!

I gulped, drew back in dismay, stumbled down the aisle, and, over the wild roar of laughter, realized that for one of the few times in my life I was speechless!

An alert master of ceremonies finds pay dirt in the simple, everyday sound of an odd name. That's why M.C.s who know their business will always try to have the volunteer give his own name; there might be a laugh scrambled among the vowels and the consonants. And it adds an element of surprise.

I wandered through the women at a "House Party" broadcast one afternoon, looking for a laugh to bolster a somewhat sagging show. It came when I least expected it.

"And what is your name?" I asked a plumpish, middle-aged woman.

"Mrs. Smell," she answered.

After a giggle from the audience, I asked if she had any little "stinkers" at home. The laugh I needed came up to my expectations. So I passed on to the next woman, sitting beside her. You can imagine what happened to the audience when she said her name was "Mrs. Sniff"! Away we went!

Personal problems, love, sickness, financial circumstances,

dreams, ambitions . . . they all parade before my microphone every day as people tell the world what's on their minds.

A woman told me she was a medical reporter in a hospital and her job required several hours of research every day in the city morgue. It seems a young intern also was doing research in that most unromantic of rendezvous. They fell in love, climaxing their courtship in a most unusual way.

"Come upstairs to the laboratory," he invited one day. "I have something I want to show you."

She complied. Her pulses quickened as the handsome young swain opened a large box and removed several pieces of a dissected human heart.

"There!" he explained proudly. "I just wanted to show you how *my* heart beats for you!"

They were married shortly after.

We picked a sailor from one side of the audience one afternoon, asked him if he was single and if he was doing anything that night.

Yes, he was single, and no, he wasn't doing anything.

Then we went over to the other side of the house and I picked out a pretty young miss. Yes, she was single, and no, she didn't have a date that night.

Anticipatory giggles raced through the audience as I introduced them to each other, asked a few questions about likes and dislikes, gave the sailor ten dollars, and cleared two seats together in the front row so they could watch the rest of the show in each other's company.

Three days later I ran into the sailor on Hollywood Boulevard. On his arm was the pretty young miss. They were engaged!

We were looking for the "Oldest Old Maid," and surprisingly enough, we found dozens of them over eighty. The winner was ninety-three, spry, witty, and a grand old lady. I noticed the laugh wrinkles about her eyes and began to kid with her. She held her own all the way. At the climax of our interview she said she not only was unwed but that she had never been kissed by anyone outside her family circle. Whereupon I leaned down and planted a smacker that shattered a record that had stood for ninety-three years. None enjoyed it more than the "Oldest Old Maid"!

It isn't all comedy that makes the "House Party" my favorite. Occasionally a story comes along, unexpectedly, that brings a lump to my throat. I'm a sucker for a good human-interest yarn.

Hearts must have skipped a beat all over America the day "Miss Johnson" turned up on our show. Her name isn't Johnson, but we'll call her that for obvious reasons.

It was a Thursday and the regular day for a visit from Caroline Leonetti, the famous charm and beauty authority on the Pacific coast. Caroline had chatted with a number of women in the audience, advising them on matters of dress and hair styles. At the conclusion of her part of the program, Caroline was to select the "glamour gal" of the week . . . some woman in the studio audience who was better groomed than all the rest: the most attractive woman present.

Without a moment's hesitation, Caroline suddenly wheeled about and pointed straight at an attractive woman in her thirties with unusual poise and dignity and good looks. The surprised winner received with great modesty the rare compliments paid by Miss Leonetti. She said her name was "Miss Johnson," and to the enthusiastic applause of four hundred other women in the audience, I awarded her an electric iron.

Two weeks later our special guest for the day was Perc Westmore, the highly successful make-up head at Warner Brothers studios and partner in the fabulous House of Westmore. Perc has an artist's flair for the dramatic and his visits to the "House Party" are always well received. Even I was unprepared for his dramatic entrance on this particular day.

"Before we go into our routine today, Art," he began, "let me tell you a little story.

"Three years ago a young woman came to see me at my

office. She was a schoolteacher, had been engaged, and had always been popular and socially prominent. Tragedy struck one day, six months before she came to see me. She had put her hair up in celluloid combs for the night. Somehow her hair had caught fire and the combs had exploded.

"All of her hair was destroyed, her face horribly blistered, and from the upper lip to the top of her head a mass of scars made her into a repulsive caricature.

"The effects of the tragedy on her mind were equally as horrible. She was virtually a psychopathic case. In desperation she appealed to me. She could no longer teach school, her fiancé had deserted her, and her friends shunned her. Believe me, it was pathetic beyond comprehension."

Perc's voice trembled as he told the story. The studio audience was strangely quiet.

"There didn't seem much I could do for her," he continued, "but she was in such terrible need for help I decided to try.

"I arranged for a meeting with a famous plastic surgeon and together we designed a new face for her. Weeks and months of painful, strenuous work by the surgeon resulted in a miracle. She began to regain the features of a normal, pretty woman. Her despair gradually faded, and at the end of a year it appeared she had won a major victory.

"I designed a complete new hairpiece for her, so delicately and expertly made as to defy detection. I had some special powders made up, for grafted skin has no pores, and a face without pores would appear at once unnatural. I showed her how to apply the make-up so none but the expert could determine what was underneath. I called in a fashion designer to advise her on the type and style of clothes that best suited her new personality."

An expectant hush fell over the audience as Perc's eyes began to glow.

"This was three years ago when the tragedy struck," he continued. "Today I'm the happiest man in Hollywood, and the proudest. For the most attractive woman in your studio audience last week, the woman who was selected by an expert above all others present, was that same 'Miss Johnson' who came to me in desperation three years ago. And here she is!"

And with that, from the wings there came a radiant, smiling "Miss Johnson."

Do you wonder why I love show business?

It's pretty difficult to talk when you have a lump in your throat. I found it so once in San Francisco.

I was standing in the lobby of the Sir Francis Drake Hotel, going over my list of interviews for the night, when I felt a tug at my elbow. I turned abruptly and there before me was a completely inconsequential-looking little fellow, about fortyish, partly balding, and whose little mild face looked up hopelessly as he said, "I want to be on your radio program, Mr. Linkletter. It's my last chance."

"What do you mean, it's your last chance?" I asked. "Your last chance to do what?"

"Well, it's kind of a long story," he began, "but I'm looking for my old sweetheart and I haven't been able to find her anywhere and I thought if you'd let me on your program, maybe she'd hear me and get in touch with me."

"I'm sorry," I brushed him off, "but the program's booked up for tonight, and anyway, I'm not running a lost-and-found department."

As I turned away I heard his wistful voice concluding, "I haven't seen her for nineteen years."

I stopped and thought that over a second and then, as its full import sunk in, I turned and exclaimed, "Nineteen years! You mean you have lost her for that long?"

"That's right," he replied. "We were sweethearts here in San Francisco nineteen years ago, but my mother got sick in the Midwest and I went back to take care of her. She promised me she'd wait for me and I swore I'd come back someday to marry her. Well, here I am, and now I can't find her."

"My God, man!" I stared at him. "That's a long time to ask anyone to wait. Besides, didn't you write or anything?"

"Well, we did for a while, but you know how those things are. She moved and I lost her address, and then one thing or another kept happening until finally nineteen years went by and here I am!"

"How long have you been in town?" I asked.

"About a week, and I haven't been able to find anyone who knew her at any of the addresses I have. You're my last chance, Mr. Linkletter!" I thought to myself, "This is really sticking out my chin, but here goes, for the helluvit." I turned and said, "Bud, you're on."

Half an hour later he was blurting out his story over KPO. Before we were off the air a bellboy came running with a message from the switchboard to say that the missing sweetheart had heard the show and was coming down to the hotel. What a reunion that was! The entire audience remained after the broadcast, awaiting the tender love scene that was to follow. The little man walked back and forth, alternately biting his fingernails and pulling the lobe of his ear viciously. What would she look like? What would she say? How would he answer?

All those things were running through my mind, too, when suddenly across the lobby and into the broadcasting studio came a pretty brunette, stylishly dressed and wreathed in nervous smiles. She was there . . . she was beautiful. He saw that, and it wrenched his heart. Nineteen years—they were ending now—nineteen thousand years!

"Virginia! Darling!"

"Fred . . . it's so nice to see you again."

"I . . . I don't know what to say."

"Fred, you're just the way I remember you."

"Virginia, you're even more beautiful than I had remembered."

"And, Fred, I'm only sorry that my husband couldn't have come with me. He had to stay home with the children!"

I never become used to the strange twists that follow many of the interviews, like one I remember during the war. A great number of mothers were engaged in defense work. As a result a community-sponsored project attempted to interest other women in caring for the defense workers' children.

I had a call from the head of this project, asking if I couldn't publicize the need for housewives to contribute time to these nurseries. Of course I was glad to co-operate and suggested she send up her best worker for a radio interview on the subject.

The very best worker turned up in a few days, and I must say she was wonderful: conscientious, hard-working, a grand speaker. All in all she put over her problem expertly and with great success.

A few days later I ran into the head of the project on the street. "Well," I began cheerfully, "how'd the broadcast go? Did we get you some volunteers?"

The woman sighed and frowned. "Yes," she answered slowly, "we have plenty of volunteers now, thanks to you. But I'll never do it again."

Puzzled, I asked her why.

"Well, the girl who you interviewed, our very best worker, thinks she's a radio star now and won't do a blessed thing. You've ruined *her* completely!"

I'm not always guilty of fracturing romances or sprinkling stardust in nurses' eyes. Sometimes they ruin themselves.

Take the charming woman who jumped to her feet eagerly when I asked for volunteers who were observing some sort of anniversary. She happily announced she'd been married that very morning. So I chose her to be on the "House Party."

A few minutes later, over the entire broadcasting facilities of the Columbia network, she again confided that she had been married that very morning and sitting down there in the sixth row was her brand-new husband. The audience applauded warmly.

Five minutes after we had concluded our broadcast, the telephone rang in the engineer's booth. It was for me. A man's voice, excited, wanted me to bring to the phone "the new bride who's just been on the air."

It was her first husband. He'd heard the program and was terribly upset, inasmuch as his ever-loving wife had neglected to divorce him before trying it again!

My Slips Were Showing

ONE OF THE BASIC REASONS FOR THE POPULARITY OF AD-LIB shows goes back to the days of the Romans, when gladiators took on lions, bears, wolves, and each other before the blood-thirsty mobs that packed the coliseums. Like the present-day crowds who jam into football stadiums, prize fights, and auto races, they wanted the morbid thrill that bloodletting inspires in so many of us.

On the air the master of ceremonies becomes the modern stand-in for the ancient gladiator; the contestant becomes the unpredictable antagonist; and the viewers are anxiously wait-ing to see who will slip and cut his throat on the camera.

Of course no one really WANTS to see the star get it in the neck (I wonder), but IF he's going to get it, everybody wants to be there to see the gore.

Broadcasters who have grown up with a script in their hands, a director to tell them when to start, speed up, slow up, or stop, and four or five hours of rehearsal back of each show are aghast at the casual manner with which I approach the show. What's going to happen? Where are you sure of getting laughs? Supposing the contestant is a jerk? What if he says something profane or dirty?

These things, somehow, don't bother me. Perhaps it's be-cause I am fatalistic. Perhaps because it doesn't do any good to worry. But more than likely it's because I've been through so many years full of so many crises that I've gained con-fidence in the knowledge that every one of the terrible things that can happen to you has already happened to me. Either I have guessed right, on the spot, and remember it because of the approval won thereby; or I've said the wrong thing and been kicked around so much I'll never forget and do it again. At any rate, the gnawing worry that you might suppose is ever-present actually is negligible.

Just the other day I was listening to a quiz show and a contestant was answering a question about Eli Whitney's cotton-gin invention. As I recall it, his words went about like this:

"After the cotton gin was invented, the work of the niggers in Southern cotton fields changed."

I waited for some kind of an explanation by the M.C. because of that word "nigger" which had been so casually dropped into the chatter.

There was none. Either he was ignorant of the insult that had just been tossed at millions of Americans, or he prayed that no one would notice it, or he didn't know how to correct the error gracefully.

I can assure you that he knows better by now, and if he has any good sense, he's busy figuring out the answer to this kind of a faux pas next time it occurs.

Two seconds after that remark went unchecked, the switchboards of every station on that network were lit up from one side to another, and bewildered operators were trying to figure out why the wrath of God was being called down upon their heads by furious listeners. The next day letters and wires would be delivered to each station elucidating in lurid detail exactly why that program and that M.C. should be removed from the air.

All this because the man at the mike did not realize that no demeaning words can ever be used on the air which directly, or inferentially, offend any race, color, or creed.

In spite of anything you might say, in warning, before air time, occasionally an unprofessional guest will commit this error.

How do you handle it? There are two definite methods.

First, the gentle, corrective substitution of the proper word, with perhaps a soft-spoken reminder that it's a more friendly and kind expression.

A woman was describing how she had first met the man she married. She explained that it had been down South and she had been on a train coming into New Orleans.

"I was getting off the car, and a nigger took my bags when—"

"I beg your pardon," I interrupted quickly. "I'm sure you meant to say a 'Negro' took your bags."

"Of course," she picked me up, blushing a trifle. "I always tell my children never to use that other word. I'm sorry."

She went on to tell her story, and the only calls or letters to come in as a result of that quick correction were congratulatory.

However, in some cases it is necessary to go much farther.

A belligerent fellow at one of my open-forum broadcasts was discussing the problem of perpetual unrest in Europe, when he said:

"If all the kikes would move to Palestine—"

"I'm sorry," I cut in strongly, "but if you want to use a word for a race or a religion, please use the proper one."

"Kike is plenty proper, to my way of thinking," he shot back.

"In that case I must apologize to my listeners for this offensive language, and that will definitely be all from the last speaker. On any program which is my responsibility, there will be affronts to no race, color or creed." And saying this, I firmly took the microphone and moved on to the next volunteer, while the audience applause threw a definite chill into any of the brash plans he might have had for carrying on.

No matter how stern the measures, the M.C. must insist upon the right to correct or bar any studio guest at the microphone.

On the subject of profanity the rules differ a little. There is still the same insistence upon proper behavior on the air, but a slip of the tongue is much more forgivable, and if it does not happen again with the same contestant, I generally do not interrupt. Only a half dozen times in nineteen years has anyone ever sworn during a broadcast of mine, and then it was only a mild "damn" or "hell."

In one instance that I can recall, a man was discussing the scariest event of his life. He had been a pilot in Italy, and he had been strafing a railroad yard when he became a victim of a rather strange malady called by the fighters "target fascination."

In this semihypnotic condition, the flyer forgets his plane, the ground, and his training as he focuses upon the target and dives relentlessly toward it.

In the case of my microphone guest, the urgent call of his wing commander pierced his trance through the radio headphones strapped to his ears. He pulled out just in time to pick up some dirt on the belly of his plane.

"Believe me, I damn near died when I realized how close I'd been."

In my judgment there was one spot where a bit of profanity could not be censored by anyone who was listening to that earnest tale.

Most people are awed by the microphone and are on their best behavior when in front of it. Unless they are completely lost in the telling of a story and lapse naturally and unconsciously into the habit of swearing, or unless they are scared by some sudden shock into profanity, they will never in the world swear during an interview.

I'll never forget an appearance on Hildegarde's show when I guested with Paramount's star, the husky-voiced Lizabeth Scott. There was a hilarious bit of tomfoolery that resulted in diapers being pinned on me, with Lizabeth feeding me marshmallows. It was to culminate with my leaping on her lap for a lullaby. The studio executives decided at the last moment that this was far, far too ludicrous for their new dramatic find, so they ordered that I should sit down on the chair beside her for the final smash laugh. This order came through one hour before air time.

I knew it was too late to rewrite the bit. Besides, without the visual picture of me on her lap, there would be no final boff. And so, conniving with Director Herb Moss and Star Hildegarde, I planned to make the leap for the lap without Lizabeth or her boss knowing about it.

The show rolled along beautifully. Unsuspectingly, Lizabeth sat down after feeding me the marshmallows. Hildegarde screamed into the mike that I had gotten just what was coming to me after all the dirty tricks I had perpetrated on my "People Are Funny" contestants.

And then I made the dive, diapers and all, for the Scott lap. Moss was just coming up with a portable microphone to hear my first words, when Lizabeth, unconscious of the mike's presence and mad as a hornet, yelled in her baritone register:

"Get off me, dammit!"

We were all saved by the grace of the studio laughter which had welled up to drown the microphone ribbon under an avalanche of sound waves. Only a few keen-eared listeners caught the slip, and they couldn't be too sure of what had actually been said.

Perhaps the most striking instance of firmness in handling a recalcitrant contestant occurred on the Midway of the Texas Centennial Exposition in Dallas. Take my word for it: Striking!

I was doing a typical man-on-the-street show for a tire company over KRLD, Dallas. The program originated right in the middle of the Fun Zone at 6 P.M. nightly. My engineer, his portable equipment, and myself completed the roster of personnel and preparation. Everything else depended upon the visitors, celebrities, and freaks from the side shows.

It was usually a lively broadcast because of the colorful conglomerate you could depend upon to be at a big fair. The only danger was from the so-called "visiting fireman" who couldn't handle his firewater. But the number of good-natured spectators always gave me a wide choice and I could steer clear of anyone who looked too congenial in a dazed sort of way.

One rainy, cold day in September, however, when we set up our remote-control microphone, there wasn't a soul to be seen. The drizzle and wind, combined with a colorless week-day attendance, had cut my interviewees down to exactly nothing.

We went on the air with a prayer for somebody, anybody, to come along. And somebody DID!

I had loafed through the opening, idled through a description of the surroundings, and was killing time kidding the engineer when around the corner staggered a character lit up like the aurora borealis.

In spite of my predicament, I couldn't take a chance on this one, so I turned my back and started to tell a story about what had happened the previous week. I had almost reached the punch line when:

"Shay. Whash goin' on round here? Broadcastin', huh?"

It was the drunk. Gay, carefree, uninhibited . . . and ill-omened! He was out for a good time, and my broadcast was going to be part of it. So I took a chance.

"What's your name, old boy?" I questioned him, with camaraderie dripping from every pore.

"Oh no, you don't." He closed one eye and shook a warning finger unsteadily at my nose. "No namesh, shee! Jush shay I'm a guy from Detroit. Good ol' town of Detroit. Who the hell're you?"

"Please!" I shook off his encircling arm. "We're on the air, and—"

The brush-off I had given his arm converted him suddenly from an amiable lush to a tough guy. He thrust his chin out under squinting brows, put his hands akimbo on hips, and muttered:

"Oh, smart guy, huh? Who'n hell yuh shovin' round, huh?"

I attempted a feeble smile and put out a hand in a gesture of conciliation.

"Look, mister, I'm just trying to earn a living doing a little broadcasting. Won't you please go away and have a good time for yourself?"

Of course I realized that this was all going out on the air. And unconsciously I was doing just the right thing in letting my listeners know my dilemma right from the start. The sympathy was all with me. No matter what he did or said now, he was definitely the "heavy."

"I oughtta knock your damn block—" he cursed at me.

I moved into the mike, my mind made up, and riding over his swearing with my own words, I explained to the listeners that there would be a short pause and not to go away because I'd be right back.

With this, I handed the microphone to my startled engineer, turned, and smashed my two hundred pounds into the obnoxious visitor. He sat down with a thump, shook his head, and when I pulled him to his feet for the clincher, he whimpered he'd had enough and slunk off down the street.

By this time a few people had appeared, and while they stared in complete disbelief, I went back to the equally startled engineer, retrieved my mike, and explained between labored breaths what had happened.

Letters of congratulation came flooding in, along with a tremendous stack of new listeners who had heard about it and wanted to be at their loud-speakers, just in case. . . .

Some of the touchiest subjects in broadcasting concern occupations. As the motion-picture people found out long ago, no villain can be engaged in any calling but that roars of protest come billowing in from those trades or professions.

The sole exception seems to be Fuller Brush men. They have been kidded for so long that they've developed an immunity. They have become insult-repellent, and, like Brooklynites, they even glory in their persecution.

Lawyers are different.

One afternoon on Market Street in San Francisco, I was busy collaring passers-by for my Gallenkamp Shoe broadcast when a siren's warning oscillation stopped traffic. Seizing this opportunity for a bit of impromptu drama, I ceased the interviews and started a special-events type of announcing:

"The great, bustling heart of the city is slowing to a stop," I almost whispered. "Down from Twin Peaks the sound of a wailing siren heralds an exciting bit of drama. Streetcars grind to a stop. Autos pull over obediently to the curb, while policemen shoo the milling spectators out of the safety zones to the sidewalks. Now we see the red light of a speeding car. Is it the fire chief on his way to a four-alarm blaze? Is it the police after a bank robber? It's almost here now!"

"Aha!" I cried triumphantly as the siren came in full blast. "It's an ambulance speeding toward Emergency. And following it at full speed is a car crowded with lawyers yelling, 'Sue! Sue! Sue!'"

I thought it was pretty funny.

But the San Francisco Lawyers' Association, meeting with Mr. Gallenkamp the next day, had a distinctly different reaction. And even my explanation that it was a car full of OAKLAND lawyers somehow left something to be desired.

What about double-entendre? The dread double meaning that plagues professional and layman alike during moments when evil is far from the mind is something impossible to make any generalizations about. It depends entirely upon who, what, and where.

If there is any over-all rule involving these unintentional cracks, it is that the listening audience will forgive almost anything if it is clearly not intended. The most sexy remark, the most improper word will get by if the listeners are convinced it is a "malaprop" or a misunderstanding.

There are many stories that could be told, and yet more which cannot be told in a book that must go through the mails. Every obscenity has at some time or another inadvertently been uttered, and yet radio goes on its merry way as essentially family entertainment.

Sometimes the performer himself is guilty of mistakes which he's not even aware of at the time. After all, when you're on a hot spot, harassed from every side, and juggling questions and answers at a mile-a-minute clip, it is understandable that from time to time there's going to be a slip-up.

My "blind spot" seems to be expectant mothers.

In spite of my familiarity with this condition, as the father of five, I never seem to notice the delicate condition of the ladies I am interviewing, and some of the things I say in perfect innocence set off gales of studio laughter that startle me out of my composure.

During a visit of the "House Party" to Fresno in 1945 I was chatting with a housewife before an audience of four or five thousand people who could plainly see that the lady was to become a mother in another two months. This rather obvious situation had escaped me completely.

"Where did you first see the man you finally married?" I inquired brightly.

"Well"—she hesitated for a moment—"as I remember it, I was backing my car out of the garage. He was walking by on the sidewalk. And I ran over him."

"What happened next?" I raised my voice over the roar of laughter.

"I took him to the hospital, where they put him in a big plaster-of-paris cast from head to foot. He had a whole lot of broken bones and had to stay there for a long, long time. But I kept visiting him and we fell in love and got married."

"Right there in the hospital?" I prodded.

"Sure!" she nodded enthusiastically. "We just couldn't wait."

"Gee, that's a swell story," I congratulated her. "But what I want to know is this: did he ever get out of the cast?"

Her answer was lost in the scream of laughter that filled the auditorium!

I didn't figure it out until Mrs. Linkletter explained the whole thing to me after the broadcast.

Then there is one other time that I remember blushingly, when I used a word carelessly that I had not taken the trouble to look up in the dictionary.

At the San Francisco World's Fair I was doing a "World's Fair Party" show each Saturday night on the Mutual Don Lee Network. I not only interviewed visitors to Treasure

Island but occasionally arranged special stunts, like a marriage on the air!

We placed ads in various newspapers, in the personal columns, asking for young couples who were willing to get married during the program from the fair. All expenses were to be paid, plus generous gifts donated from exhibits and concessions.

A young couple was finally located and all arrangements were completed for the following week's broadcast. And so, at the conclusion of the program, I triumphantly forecast the next show:

"Don't miss next Saturday night's program . . . when right here on the stage before our Mutual microphones . . . a happy young couple will consummate their marriage vows."

Wow! What an audience we had!

One of the most common errors of beginning M.C.s—or, for that matter, any interviewer who is not alert—is putting words into contestant's mouths and denying them the opportunity to express themselves.

Recently a famous comedian substituted for an ad-lib man, and I was astounded to hear him fall right into the mistake of anticipating every possible sentiment of his guest.

"I see by your card that you are Mrs. John Smith. Right?" he began.

"Yes, that's right," Mrs. Smith answered.

"I suppose you're a housewife," the star went on.

"Yes." She nodded.

"Uh-huh. I understand you're from Denver, Colorado. Wonderful town, isn't it?"

"Wonderful," she agreed again.

He was getting a little desperate now. "I'll bet you're having a marvelous vacation in Hollywood, seeing all the sights?"

"Oh yes!" she agreed enthusiastically.

At this point he gave up and went into a prepared routine, feeling, undoubtedly, that here was a really stupid woman who couldn't say anything. When, as a matter of fact, he hadn't given her the CHANCE.

Not too long ago, in a moment of mental doldrums, I fell into this same rut on the "House Party." We had selected the most recently married couple for an interview, and as they approached the mike my mind was occupied with wondering about another part of the show yet to come.

"So you're the most recently married couple at the 'Party' today," I began explanatorily.

"That's right," the groom replied.

"Been married for just one week, isn't that so?" I filled in.

"That's right," he agreed.

"I suppose you had a big church wedding with friends and relatives all there to see you march down the aisle?"

"That's right," he approved.

"And after the wedding you had a reception with all the trimmings?" By this time I had ceased to think mechanically and was beginning to realize how stupidly the interview was going. I thought, "Linkletter, you dope, get on the ball."

"That's right," he was answering for the fourth time as I reproached myself bitterly. THIS time I'd get something from him or know the reason why.

"And WHAT did you do after the reception?" I inquired innocently.

The burst of laughter from the studio audience and the embarrassed silence from the couple shocked me into the realization that here was an unanswerable question . . . on the air.

Of course I wiggled out of it by picking up the conversational thread quickly: "I mean, where did you go on your honeymoon?" But the harm had been done, and from that moment on nothing could be said that sounded innocent, for once an audience gets into a playful mood of interpreting every word in the manner of the double-entendre, heaven help the poor performer.

In passing, I'd like to mention another faux pas which is

sometimes made and which would never sink in unless he read the mail or answered the phones AFTER he had made it. I am speaking of allusions to the Bible, or passages out of it used in a kidding way.

No matter how careful you are in your choice, the church people of the United States (and there are millions) resent any reference to the Scriptures. I was reminded of this recently when I made such a slip while chatting with five youngsters on my "House Party" show. They were five and six years of age, and a more blissfully innocent-looking group of curly-headed angels I have never seen. It was just before Thanksgiving, and among other topics I brought up the subject of preparing the holiday meal and how they would go about it.

"First," I said, "we must kill the turkey. What's the best way?"

"Shoot it through the eyes with a shotgun!" screamed one little girl.

"Wring its neck!" offered another of the cherubs.

"Stab it in the stomach with a knife!" giggled a third.

"Cut its head off!" cooed a five-year-old.

By this time the audience was almost in hysterics at the sight of these naïve, trusting youngsters prescribing such bloodcurdling deaths for a turkey. A phrase flashed through my mind which is always associated with the innocence of babes, and I said:

"Suffer the little children to come unto me. . . ."

And while most of the letters and calls were kindly in nature, they were definitely critical of such a transposition . . . and rightly so.

The wonder of it is that, with so many split-second decisions to make every minute that we're on the air, there are not MORE slips made.

As I say in reply to the question "How do you think of so many things to ask so fast?", it isn't just what you *hear* that an M.C. thinks of, but the other three things that he thought of and discarded before he hit on the RIGHT question that makes this business so speedy.

I blush to recall the unforgettable moment when I committed my most embarrassing slip.

I was interviewing a handsome redheaded young fellow of seven. Somehow he reminded me of someone I knew. We had discussed his hobbies, games, and pets. Almost as an afterthought I inquired, "And what does your mother do?"

"She works in the homes of movie stars writing letters."

"Oho!" I enthused, sensing I had struck pay dirt. "And what famous stars employ your mother for this private secretarial work?"

"Dorothy Lamour, Betty Hutton, Red Skelton—"

"Red Skelton!" I interrupted as I suddenly recognized the resemblance. "Say! You know *you* look just like Red—"

My voice choked off as I, and the whooping audience along with me, suddenly realized the significance of my observation.

I said the wisest thing in the world in explanation.

Nothing.

The Postman Rings More Than Twice

TWENTY YEARS AGO WHEN A LISTENER MAILED A COMplaining letter to a radio program, everybody from the assistant producer to the sponsor went into a tizzy. Every letter arriving at a broadcasting station was read and reread to find out about the popularity of programs and stars. This was in the days before so-called "rating services" sprang into existence and "Nielsens" and "ARB's" established a popularity level for each program.

Today letters are still important, but they no longer assume the exaggerated importance of yesterday. We have come to realize that in an audience numbering scores of millions, people take shows for granted; they'll turn off a program if they don't like it, but will seldom bother to sit down and write one way or another. In this tremendous audience there is a percentage of cranks, crackpots, and chronic grouches, whose only joy in life appears to be picking their fellow men apart. Yet most big programs spend large sums of money and time in carefully answering every question or complaint. Red Skelton, for example, goes so far as to keep a cross-indexed file of all names and addresses of people who have written him, and on appropriate holidays he will send a broadside message to all of them. Fan-letter-writing services have sprung up in Hollywood and New York which, for a certain fee, will handle all fan mail of a program and send appropriately autographed postcards or letters in return.

This is possible because nearly all fan mail can be divided quickly into seven categories.

First, the gush fan, who is overwhelmed by some special mention of her home town or her hobby or a relative, and who writes to say how much pleasure the mention gave her. Second, there is the begging letter. It asks for help in getting a job, an apartment, doctor bills paid, college expenses sustained, or for food and clothing. Third, there is the letter which attempts to win a prize or get money by suggesting something the program can do, such as a certain question or stunt or guest. Fourth, the letter asking for autographed pictures and personal souvenirs from the stars, such as old neckties, handkerchiefs, and lucky pieces. Fifth, the grumpy letters complaining about the star's attitude, manner, speech, the program's pace, content, style, the sponsor's product or dealers. Sixth, the letters asking for tickets. These may come in from any part of the United States; many people seem to think the program is originating in their own home town even though frequent mentions are made of Hollywood or New York, whichever the case might be. And finally, the majority of nice, friendly letters from folks who liked the broadcast and simply want you to know it.

One woman writes me each year for my autograph on a piece of pink paper which she sends me. This, she writes, she keeps under her pillow each night. Apparently it wears out in the course of a year. Another gal wrote for my autograph on a piece of material which she said she would embroider over with a different colored thread and piece it to a quilt she was making up. She wanted to sleep under her favorite stars! Another wrote and asked if I wouldn't please send her a wooden leg, in return for which she would tell everyone wherever she went that my program was the donor!

One of the most startling letters ever to arrive in my mail came from an institution for the mentally unbalanced outside of Chicago. You could never tell this from the dignified letterhead, which indicated that it was an estate for wealthy vacationers. At any rate, this letter read:

DEAR MR. LINKLETTER,

I'm writing you because you are the only one who can help me. There is nothing wrong with me except that I'm in love with Joan Davis and they won't let me out of here to come to California and marry her. I listen to your programs every day and I know from your voice that I can trust you. I have friends in Chicago who will help get me out of here. Please contact them immediately and do something about this.

I have tried to write to Joan but they catch me and tear up the letters before I can mail them, so I have written her a special letter and I hope you will give it to her the next time you see her. Don't worry, I'll see that you get plenty when I get out. I am rich and have my money all hidden in old tomato cans up in the hills. Your pal.

(Signed)

The letter to Joan was an ardent love letter:

DEAR JOAN,

If you have listened when you are on the radio you know that I love you because every week when I have your program on and you stop talking I tell you through the loud-speaker that I want to marry you, but you never say anything back to me. Is this because of some ruling on the radio? They won't let me write you and they tear up all my letters, but don't worry, I'm all right and I'll get out of here and come to California and find you. Love and kisses.

When I showed this to Joan and she read that last sentence, I'm sure it did her peace of mind no good for the next few weeks.

The letter that takes top honors in my files is the one from a lady in Dallas, Texas, who wrote as follows:

DEAR MR. PEOPLE ARE FUNNY:

You don't know who is writing this letter and you'll never find out. It is the first letter I have ever written to a radio program and it will probably be the last.

But I want you to know that you have just saved my life!

I'm a widow whose two sons have been killed in the war; the first one in training when his plane crashed, the second who died in Normandy and whose death I have just learned about today. They were the only reason for my living and when the War Department notified me this afternoon of Michael's death I decided I couldn't go on alone. With strips of adhesive tape I sealed up the windows and doors of my little kitchen and got ready to turn on the gas. My radio was on to the war news which made me feel even more bitter and determined to go through with it, but just as I had almost gotten to turning on the gas your program came on the air. I started to turn it off because the thought of so many people laughing and enjoying life was unbearable to me, but somehow I didn't. Maybe it was the ironic thought that I'd die while listening to other people living that kept my fingers from the dial.

Then suddenly something happened to me. I began to listen to a crazy stunt you had where a woman and her husband went out with a covered bird cage inside of which you had locked an alarm clock which would go off when they were in the middle of a big restaurant. I had to know how they came out, so I listened on. In the next fifteen or twenty minutes that gaiety and fun of your show did things to me. I can't explain it, except that I didn't turn on the gas and when you finally finished, I knew that I could never do what I planned.

It is morning now and before I go to work and try to fill up my life with things to make me forget Michael and Bob, I wanted to take this minute to let you know that somewhere in Texas a woman lives because people are funny.

Gratefully,
(Signed)

Strange are the requests which pour across a broadcaster's desk from frantic, desperate listening "friends." Here is one, written simply and humbly, in a hand that is firm and true. It tells far better than most how forsaken and helpless a human being can become. It was written from Oneonta, New York, and it began with no preamble, no excuses:

DEAR SIR:

I am writing you to see if you will help us to find someone who would adopt the baby I am expecting any day, and would pay my hospital and doctor bill. I cannot afford another baby. We have four other children, ages 13, 11, 7, and 4. I haven't even got any baby clothes for the next one yet. We have just moved into this house recently, and there are so many things I need to make the house livable and the children need so many things to wear that I don't know what I will do when the new one arrives. My husband is a good steady worker, but it takes all of his wages to pay the many bills that we owe. I am not well and the only convenience we have is electric lights. We have to get our water from a well and we don't have gas, so you see it is rather hard on me. If you will mention about the baby on the air, please don't mention my name. Hoping to hear from you real soon. Sincerely . . .

This sort of letter, read on the air, would be a bombshell for our overworked staff of girls. At least ten thousand replies would come flooding in within two days after this case received network publicity, and our responsibility would be further complicated by the fact that we would know nothing about the background of the case or the legal aspects of adoption in the state of New York. And so, regretfully, I declined. We referred her request to the manager of the local network station and asked him to see the proper authorities in the local Community Chest for help and financial assistance.

One of my favorite fan letters came from a listener in Sioux City, Iowa. She wrote:

DEAR MR. LINKLETTER:
  People Are Funny, but you aren't!

Anyone who has a sensitive soul had better stay off the air or develop calluses quickly. The brickbats fly freely around the head of anyone brash enough to try to entertain millions of people with one brand of humor or drama or news. Out of any cross section of listeners, you are lucky to be able to please half, and of the remaining fifty per cent there will be some who not only are indifferent but who take a lively dislike to your particular personality . . . and tell you about it!

Most of these "poison-pen" letter writers prefer to remain safely anonymous—not only because of libel laws, but because of certain U. S. Postal Department rules against obscenity in the mails—but I'll never forget one who had the nerve to sign his disparaging notes.

His first one was sent directly to the Columbia Broadcasting System, Hollywood. It was directed to the President in Charge of Programs, and it said among other things:

  Of all the stupid, inane, obnoxious, and insulting

people on the air, this Linkletter who spouts every afternoon over your network is the most moronic, imbecilic,
and infantile so-called master of ceremonies I've ever
heard. Why don't you get somebody *intelligent* to interview the asinine women who subject themselves to his
insults.

This touching tribute to my ability was promptly turned
over to me by the CBS fan-mail department with several
ribald remarks penciled in the margin by my pals at the
network. After a generous circulation among my colleagues,
that letter was tacked up on my office wall as a reminder
that "you can fool some of the people . . ." et cetera.

The next letter from this ardent fan came to me by way
of the Federal Communications Commission in Washington,
D. C., who thought I might enjoy its fond sentiments. It
read in part:

Such broadcasts by Linkletter prove to me that the
Government of the United States is not taking seriously
the job of censoring the air waves that belong to the
people. I am enclosing a letter from my Senator advising
me to get in touch with you about radio complaints, and
I wish you would take action immediately to bar this
clod-pated dope from future broadcasting.

But the letter which finally prompted me to action was
a letter to the General Electric Company, at that time my
sponsor. That one found my Achilles' heel. It read:

I am personally encouraging my friends not to buy
your products until Linkletter is taken off the air. He
couldn't sell bread to starving Greeks, and as long as
he represents you with his gabble, gabble, gabble every
day, I'm never going to buy a nickel's worth of your
stuff.

Finally I got a Los Angeles city directory and looked up his name, discovered his address, and prepared myself for a person-to-person broadcast at his home.

I decided to go by in the afternoon, since he apparently was at home every day to listen to the broadcasts and pick out a different item to blast in each letter. And I also decided to pretend that I was representing a Public Opinion Poll from door to door, until I got a good look at him and sized him up for possible further action.

It was with considerable trepidation that I finally stopped before the modest white California stucco bungalow and walked up to the door. As I rang the bell I was trying to remember if I couldn't possibly have a date somewhere else that I should attend to. But then the door opened suddenly, and before me was standing a little, bespectacled fellow in his forties, with a peculiar look on his face. Before I could launch into my phony explanation, he blurted out in a scared kind of voice:

"You're Art Linkletter!"

"Yes, I am," I confessed rather strongly. Noting his size and age carefully, I went on forcefully: "And I've come to see you about those letters you've been writing."

He gulped, backed up a step or two, and then, seeming to make up his mind to a definite course of action, he waved me in and said, "Oh yes, of course. The letters . . ."

As I walked through the door a very ordinary living room confronted me, filled with the usual overstuffed chair, sofa, worn carpet, and scratched upright piano.

But . . . what was that standing on the piano? A big framed picture of—No! It couldn't be! But it was—a grinning portrait of the "clod-pated dope," Art Linkletter.

I turned back from the picture with what must have been an asinine expression and started to question him about what in hell's name—

"Wait a minute, Mr. Linkletter, and I'll tell you the whole

story." He motioned to an easy chair and started out of the room. "I'll get you a beer. Just a minute."

While he was gone I sat there figuring a hundred wild stories; but I missed the truth by a million miles.

"I want you to know there was nothing personal intended in those letters," he began. "It isn't as if I personally don't like you or your work on the air—"

"Nothing PERSONAL!" I laughed. "Like 'stupid,' 'moronic,' 'infantile,' and—"

"Please, let me explain," he begged. "Those are just words I used to try to get you off the air."

"But why in the world do you want me off the air?" I shook my head dizzily. "I have a wife, kids, a mortgage, and a desire to make a living like anyone else."

"I'm sorry"—and I could see he was genuinely contrite—"but I was driven to it by my wife!" The words came tumbling out now.

"I'm a writer without a job. In Hollywood that's not good. And especially with an ambitious wife who wants to go places and do things. Instead, she's stuck at home with two children, no help, and a radio that goes continually. About a year ago she came across your program on the air and ever since my life isn't worth the powder to blow it to hell. Day and night, night and day, she rants and raves about you. She nags me about how you use words and what's the matter with me. She compares your picture, that she got and put on the piano there, with me. She tells me what you said and how you said it and why you said it and why can't I say things like that. Then—"

"Brother, I don't blame you!" I held up my hand to stop the torrent of words. "It's a wonder you didn't come down and shoot me. I don't know what I can do to help you, but believe me, with a wife like that, you're entitled to write a letter a day!"

The visit must have done something. I've never heard from him again.

But I keep looking in the papers for a story of a shooting. . . .

Instead of telling you about the letters that come in to radio characters, let's read a few from actual writers quoting everything but names.

DEAR ART:

Maybe you didn't know this, but you have something unusual in your voice that nobody else on the radio has. I am a veterinarian and run a big dog hospital here in Chicago, and while I'm working I play the radio good and loud. When you come on the air every day at three o'clock every darned dog in the place starts to howl. Can you please explain this?

DEAR ART LINKLETTER:

I heard you mention on your program that you have a Collie dog named King. If you will send me the date of his birth, I will send you his Horoscope. Every living thing has a Horoscope of some kind, and my specialty is dogs. Once you know what the stars say about your dog he will be much more valuable in every way, and you will be another of those rare masters in harmony with the astral vibrations of your pet.

DEAR SIR:

I note that on your programs you are looking for funny special stunts to do. I hereby submit my idea for something new. You ask your audience if there are any expectant mothers there. This will enable you to have some very funny interviews with people who volunteer and you might even have them stand up and have other people guess when and how long before the baby arrives. Then, following this, you give them each ballet slippers and tell them you are going to have a dancing contest. Yrs. very truly.

DEAR MR. RADIO ANNOUNCER:

You are the freshest, breeziest bastard on the radio. In fact, I could go so far as to say: the only announcer with sex. Today we must have sex or we are sunk. Women must get it somehow. Often the busy businessman leaves the little woman alone, so alone. That's where you and your morning program comes in. The little woman, subconsciously, of course, can stand her businessman's husband's neglect more easily. You have satisfied her. And what woman would not rather be satisfied thoroughly mentally than be run over by a truck in person? Inadvertently, it is the men that should thank you, even more than your avid womanish audience.

These little facts I am pointing out are man to man. I am a woman, however, but a woman that speaks on the man-to-man basis and still stays quite a woman has it over her lesser sisters. Anyway, I hand it to you. To me the radio is a little box full of music if you turn it to the right places. I take a vicious delight in cutting off talk. Even the President of the United States. You see, I can read.

On Washington's Birthday, I was balancing my first cup of coffee when the music stopped and you came on and I had to listen while changing hands or spill my coffee in bed. Then suddenly my frustration pricked up its ears and started drinking you in. Not what you were saying. But the something you throw right into a bedroom that isn't decent so early in the A.M. And whether you stand with your female audience in the kitchen with the morning dishes, in the living room with a vacuum cleaner picking up the week-end debris, or in a bedroom with a woman making life bearable again with three cups of coffee . . . your effect is still the same: You have the old law of supply and demand by the throat.

Your cussedness of delightful assurance on the unstable ground you tread is a constant urge to every female to tear your eyes from their sockets. And here's one woman you ain't foolin', brother Linkledder. Is that how you spell your name?

I wonder what you'll do about this letter. It certainly has no place in your life. You cannot dispose of it in that "homely, chatty, informative" little category you keep by your side to make you safe, much like a cheesy private detective packs a gat while slavering over the details he is collecting for a slimy divorce trial. Damn you. . . .

Then there's the listener who wants to invent a special "code" just for her.

DEAR ART:

I belong to a club where a bunch of us housewives get together and play bridge and gossip. I told them that when I was in Hollywood I met you and we are good friends and they think I am a liar. Well, Art, I know you are a good-enough sport to help me out so here's my idea. On next Wednesday's "House Party," you get a woman up for an interview and tell her: "I'll bet I can guess your first name: Henrietta!" See, Art, this is my name, and before you go on the air, I'll tell the girls that you are going to do this as a way of saying "hello" to me. Will you, please, Art? Gee, what a thrill it will be for all of us. Thanks a million. P.S.: I am going to buy a General Electric refrigerator, maybe. It's up to you.

DEAR MR. LINKLETTER:

I am a housewife that loves to have fun, play practical jokes on all my friends, and give parties. Everybody says I am the most cuckoo person they know and why don't I be a guest on your program. I live right here in

Los Angeles and could come to NBC any time you say and would be willing to do anything for a laugh. Just because I am a woman do not think I can't take it like anyone else. You can hit me in the face with a pie, dress me up like a goof, or anything is O.K. with me.

My telephone number is —— and you can call me any time before four o'clock when my husband gets home. I don't want him to know because he might object, and besides it would be a good joke and a big surprise on him when he heard me over the radio. Here's hoping you'll be calling me right away because I'm just dying to prove that I'm as funny as people.

Variations of the above letter are placed on my desk every morning. Businessmen, tourists, high-school kids, and assorted working girls are apparently so anxious to appear on the program that they will take time to write long, pleading letters outlining their qualifications as good sports.

Invariably, however, we turn them all down with "thank-you" letters which point out that nothing is prearranged, including the contestants on our program.

DEAR ART:

Just couldn't pass up the chance to drop this one in your mailbag. A WAC was walking through the field one day and she came to a nice little pond surrounded by bushes and decided she'd take a swim. She took off her clothes and hung them on the bushes and just as she was getting her toes wet, a voice from the woods boomed out: "Camouflage Division No. 19, Forward March!" and all the little bushes got up and marched off. Do you believe that? Let's hear it on your next program.

And finally, a typical letter from a bobby-soxer.

DEAR ARTHUR:

I hope you could read the letter I sent you yesterday because I was so excited from getting your picture I couldn't write straight. Its so nice to look on the wall and see you anytime I want. I heard you twice yesterday. You were positively swoony. Doesn't your wife just about faint when she sees you? I just about do when looking

at your picture. My girl friends are going to see Van Johnson this afternoon. They all just love him but I told them I'd rather stay home and write to you. My grandmother yells at me every time I turn the radio on because I turn it on whenever I'm home. And you're the only one that she'll listen to, and considering how old she is thats surprizing because most old ladies like Tom Breneman. You're sure awfully lucky to be married because if you weren't I'd Hitch Hike or something but as long as you're married I'll just stay in Detroit and write you hundreds of letters. I guess you must send out thousands of letters every day but theres probably no one who likes you as much as I do outside of your wife and your mother. I don't see how you can be both sharp and beautiful too. Most people are either sharp and not beautiful or beautiful and not sharp except me and i guess i'm not either. My girlfriend said I shouldn't have sent you that picture of me because i've got my brothers old shirt on but I really don't look much better dressed up—well that's all I can write, right now because I always make my letters to thick and the postman brings them back.

Lots of Love

from

MARY

Detroit, Mich.

"Through the Looking Glass"

TELEVISION HAS DONE MORE TO CHANGE THE LIVING HABITS of America than any other single invention, with the exception of the automobile. Today, more people spend more time looking into the twenty-one-inch lighted screen than they do at any other occupation during their leisure time. What they see there proves that People Are Funny.

The human weakness for fads is demonstrating itself all over again, as it has done in movies, books, and on the stage. Shoot-em-up Western melodramas are littering the living rooms of America with dead cowboys and Indians. The whining ricochets of bullets from the blunt muzzles of guns aimed by private eyes and desperate gangsters raise goose pimples on the necks of quiet family folk from coast to coast, while variety and comedy shows trade guest stars each week in a repetitious game of five-figure musical chairs. And, naturally, there are "The Late Late Shows"!!

It's impossible, of course, for three networks and hundreds of independent stations to fill eighteen hours a day, seven days a week with different, fresh, and top-grade entertainment. There are not enough stars, stories, or ideas to begin to answer the demands of television.

Ten short years ago, when TV first broke through the costly technical curtain and became a mass-produced electronic miracle, the performers had only to be seen to be enjoyed. The feeblest efforts to please brought applause. A low-cut gown on a well-stacked girl made her singing voice or acting ability merely incidental. A hastily rewritten burlesque black-out, cleaned up for the family trade, was laughed at all over again. Well-thrown pies and sharply aimed seltzer water were enough for the stunt shows. And simple one-walled sets sufficed for dramatic hours.

For a few brief years, the hypoed quiz shows knocked off all the rating leaders on TV. Sweating, grimacing shoemakers, jockeys, teachers, and even moppets were locked in a variety of "isolation booths" and tempted to joggle their "photographic" minds for hundreds of thousands of dollars. This fad, too, vanished—hastened, of course, when a disgruntled loser "blew the whistle" on the methods of screening and rigging contestants—and the networks cut back on most of the big-money shows.

And still "People Are Funny" continues on the air, after nineteen years of constant effort to come up each week with fresh surprises, new games, amusing gimmicks, and above all, warmly interesting guests.

Looking back over this record-breaking run, I can recall some of the highlights of a quarter-century of proving that People Are Funny.

The most spectacular stunt was pulled on an unsuspecting married couple whose house we stole while they were out of town for a week end. Actually, we had arranged the hoax over a four-month period, before air time. We had found a vacant frame bungalow which was on a street destined to become a freeway. Knowing that the owner would eventually have to pay for its removal or take a cut in the money the city would pay him for it, we made secret arrangements to do with it what we wished. Then we set up a rental office just for the purpose of advertising this one house, screening possible "renters" and picking our pigeons for the best possible use on the show. We then rented it to the couple of our choice for a very reasonable figure, set our trap to get them out of town for a week end, and schemed to have them come to the program directly from the airport following their return to Hollywood. I then "innocently" picked them out of the studio audience and offered them a possible five hundred dollars if they had not forgotten to lock doors, close windows, turn off taps, etc., etc., during their week end away from home. When they were finally driven out to their house and saw an empty lot with only pipes sticking out of the foundations, you can imagine their consternation.

We had them on the go, looking for their house for the next five weeks via helicopter, police prowl car, and through the "Missing House" want-ad columns. Finally, they were advised to seek the help of a fortuneteller in a nearby carnival, and when they entered her huge tent . . . their house was sitting there before their startled eyes!

Of course, they enjoyed this huge joke, and their enjoyment was enhanced even more when they got a house rent-free for a year, and a variety of other choice prizes!

My outstanding interview of a famous personality was with Cecil B. De Mille. He was an intriguing mixture of actor, salesman, producer, preacher, student, and raconteur. During a four-minute interview, completely unrehearsed and impromptu, he had the audience in laughter at the mishaps he had experienced during the filming of *The Ten Commandments,* and moments later they were in tears at the reverent, touching description of Christmas in the Holy Land. He was truly one of the finest guests ever to face the microphones with me in a quarter-century of broadcasting.

The biggest prize ever given away on "People Are Funny" was a glacier. My partner-producer John Guedel had gone to Alaska one summer for a vacation, and while there bought a glacier two miles long, a mile wide, and about a half-mile deep. It was nothing but a mass of snow-covered ice that filled a huge valley from side to side. We secured a bill of sale for this and presented it to an astonished housewife in our audience, along with a note from the owner of the valley insistently requesting that the new owner get the glacier off his property by the following spring. We then pointed out that if the glacier were moved, floated down the coast to Los Angeles, and cut up for resale to icehouses, it would be worth approximately eight million dollars if ice were only five cents a pound. However, I took the whole thing off her hands, at the last second, with a generous offer of a hundred dollars!

Television is changing with each season. It is becoming more sophisticated, more polished, and more ingenious. More and more money is being spent to get bigger and better productions before the cameras. World-wide program plans are pushing the studio walls back to include entertainment from Japan, Turkey, and Russia.

But nothing will change human nature.

The little square of glass on your television receiver will never replace the little square of glass over the dressing table. The Greatest Show on Earth will still be available twenty-four hours a day in the mirrors of America.

Take another look and you'll agree: People Are Funny!